101

FIN
B
O

ACEBACK BUNCH PLAYS

Featuring 101 Game-Tested Play-Action and Run Plays from the Bunch Formation

Leo Hand

ISBN: 1-58518-913-8
Library of Congress Control Number: 2004112388
Book layout and diagrams: Deborah Oldenburg
Cover design: Jeanne Hamilton
Front cover photo: Jonathan Daniel/Getty Images

Coaches Choice
P.O. Box 1828
Monterey, CA 93942
www.coacheschoice.com

Dedication

To four generations of beautiful Navajo women:
Julia, Mary, Philomena, Faith Marie and Hope Rene

*May the Creator's breath support your wings,
and the eagle's spirit forever guide your paths.*

Ayoi a niishni

Acknowledgments

Thanks to Tony Shaw, for giving me the opportunity to coach in Texas.

Thanks to Allan Sepkowitz for giving me the opportunity
to coach at Andress High School.

Thanks to the wonderful people of the Zuni and Navajo Nations, who taught
me much more than I taught them during the seven years I lived with them.

Thanks to Joe Griffin, for giving me one of the best coaching jobs in California.

Thanks to all of the splendid young men whom I have been privileged to coach.

Thanks to all of the great coaches whom I have been fortunate
to have worked with and coached against.

Thanks to Sam Snoddy, for his assistance during this project.

Thanks to the offspring whose ancestors endured the *Middle Passage*
and the *Long Walk*, for all of the contributions that they have made
to the greatest game of all.

Thanks to Howard Wells, for giving me the chance to coach at El Paso High School.

Thanks to Herman Masin, editor of *Scholastic Coach,* for all of his help
and suggestions during the past 30 years.

Thanks to Dr. James A Peterson, and all the wonderful people at Coaches Choice,
for all of their help and encouragement.

Contents

Preface

My offense owes much to the past. There are elements such as the man-in–motion that go way back to Clark Shaughnessy's years at Stanford, a half-century ago. The basic ballhandling techniques come from Davey Nelson's winged-T at Delaware, as relayed to me through Rocky Carzo, a fellow assistant when I was at Cal in the early '60s.

The biggest influence on me was the Raider system that I learned as an assistant in 1966—and that system emanated from Sid Gilman, who probably learned from Shaughnessy and ... well, you get the picture.[1]

–Bill Walsh

Today, teams are passing the ball better than they ever have, but many modern offenses (particularly aceback offenses) fall apart when they are confronted by situations in which they must run. The purpose of this book is to incorporate some *old school* wisdom into the modern aceback running game. Because the aceback bunch formation forces a defense to defend 10 gaps and cover the four receivers who are aligned on, or near, the line of scrimmage, it has unlimited (but frequently unexplored) running game potential. This book will present 101 sequential aceback run/play-action pass plays. It will not touch upon the dropback passing game. Coaches Andrew Coverdale and Dan Robinson wrote an exceptional book, *The Bunch Attack: Using Compressed Formations in the Passing Game*, on this subject in 1997.

In an attempt to maintain coherency, all 101 plays will be initially illustrated against a 3-4 defense, but the book's final chapter will provide diagrams illustrating how each play's blocking assignments adapt to six of the most commonly used defenses in football today.

All of the plays in this book will feature a true aceback alignment. They will not feature plays in which the aceback is aligned in a fullback position such as wing-T adaptations, the flex bone (also referred to as the ham bone and triple shoot), or Don Markham's double-wing. These offensives already exemplify many of the concepts that will be presented in this book.

The catalyst that caused me to write this book is the countless conversations I have had with many young coaches regarding the offensive running game. In these conversations, I have often talked about old school tactics that have historically powered some of football's premier ground games. Unfortunately, most of these tactics have been forgotten by many of us who were fortunate enough to have witnessed them. Worse yet, a new generation of coaches have not had the opportunity to see Bud Wilkinson's split–T, Darrell Royal's wishbone, Vince Lombardi's Green Bay sweep, Woody Hayes's robust attack, John McKay's I, or Eddie Robinson's wing-T. The only types of running games they have ever seen are the ones that are presently in vogue, and many of these often leave a great deal to be desired.

Many coaches did not take the running game very seriously at one time in history. One man changed that type of thinking. Somehow, numerous coaches have again forgotten the important lessons that he taught. Hopefully, this book will stimulate thought and help Aceback coaches, young and old, develop explosive running games that will be as lethal as their passing games.

> *When I first came into this league and after I had spent all those months studying the movies, it seemed to me that while the passing game was great, the running game was like a half try. In those days everybody was saying you just couldn't sustain a running game against the pros, that their defenses were too large and too mobile. Well, they're still large and mobile today. What they forgot was that everything in football, as in physics is relative, and that the people you could put on offense could be every bit as big and just as mobile as the people on defense.[2]*

> *–Vince Lombardi*

1. Bill Walsh with Glenn Dickey. *Building a Champion: On Football and the Making of the 49ers.* (New York: St. Martin's Press, 1990). p. 33.

2. Vincent Lombardi (George L. Flynn, Ed.). *Vince Lombardi on Football.* (New York: New York Graphic Society, 1973). Vol. 1, p. 108.

1

Key Elements of Every Great Offense

Any serious student of the game knows that football coaches change their offensive schemes and philosophies almost as frequently as a teenager changes the radio station. What is *in* today will probably be *gone* tomorrow. A few years ago, many younger colleagues thought that the empty formation was the ultimate revolution in the modern game. Little did they know that Dutch Meyer was using empty sets back in the 1940s and 1950s at TCU.

Despite their fugacious nature, many offensive schemes and philosophies have endured the test of time and have thereby attained greatness. Thirty-five years of coaching, and searching for the ingredients that enable an offense to achieve greatness, have resulted in the following 23 key elements of *every* great offense. A great offense:

- Accommodates the needs of a wide variety of personnel. A coach does not have to abandon a great offense simply because he does not have an outstanding quarterback, running back(s), etc.

- Is neither inherently a passing offense nor a running offense.

- Is not a collage of randomly selected formations and plays; every component of a great offense has a specific purpose.

- Has the ability to shift gears; it has the capacity to grind it out and consume giant chunks of time, or to strike quickly and come from behind.

- Is equally effective anywhere on the field. A coach does not have to abandon a great offense simply because he is inside his opponent's 10-yard line.
- Can function in any type of weather condition.
- Does not require a weekly game plan; it is a comprehensive game plan, capable of immobilizing any defense.
- Has the ability to manipulate any defense; it can dictate fronts, adjustments, pass coverage, and styles of defensive play.
- Has the ability to destroy defensive keys and reads by double-binding defenders (double-binding means placing a defender in a no-win, "damned if he does, damned if he doesn't" situation).
- Has the ability to double-team exceptional defensive players.
- Is not predictable.
- Has the ability to provide a team with the most appropriate offensive weapon for any circumstance.
- Provides its linemen with inclusive blocking assignments that enable them to always know who they will block.
- Has a variety of blocking schemes for each different defense.
- Has a passing game that will enable it to attack any type of coverage.
- Has the ability to create 1-1 situations in the passing game and also to isolate a good receiver versus a weak defensive back.
- Has a passing game that enables receivers to adjust their pass routes when a defense disguises its coverage.
- Has the ability to outnumber the defense at the point of attack.
- Employs *real* misdirection.
- Does not expect one player to be the only ballcarrier in the running game.
- Has the ability to give its players equalizers when they are out-manned. Equalizers come in many forms. The manipulative use of formations, shifting, and motion; the passing game; the option; misdirection; sequential organization of plays; and blocking schemes that double-bind, double-team, and double-cross defenders are just a few.
- Has the ability to call and change plays at the line of scrimmage.
- Employs at least one *trademark play*, a play that every defensive opponent knows it must stop if it is to be successful. A great offense has calculated in advance all of the tactics that a defense might employ to stop its trademark play(s) and knows exactly how it will counter all of these tactics.

Common Errors that Aceback Teams Frequently Make

- Assigning 90 to 100 percent of the responsibility for the running game to one player—the aceback. A team can get away with this tactic if it has a super back like John Riggins or Terrell Davis, but it seldom works with an average or slightly above average aceback—especially when an exceptional quarterback is not backing up the aceback.

- Limiting the blocking schemes. Many aceback teams use zone blocking, and counter trey blocking, almost exclusively for their run offense. Although the implementation of two or three blocking schemes simplifies offensive line play, it also makes defensive play recognition much simpler. Furthermore, zone blocking or counter trey blocking neither double-binds nor double-crosses defenders.

- Employing little or no misdirection. Misdirection is one of the most potent offensive weapons in football. Because it creates confusion, misdirection also abates defensive aggressiveness. Having an aceback step right before he runs left is not misdirection. Misdirection occurs when the defense, the referees, the cameramen, and the fans are all trying to figure out who has the ball.

- Allowing the defenses to line up, wind up, and tee off. By limiting misdirection and limiting blocking patterns, many aceback teams enhance defensive aggression by simplifying play recognition.

- Focusing too much on the pass and not enough on the run. The pass is, without a doubt, an extremely powerful offensive weapon, but in many instances an offense must be able to run the ball. Possessing only the ability to pass the ball makes any offense one-dimensional and easier to defend. Bill Walsh, one of the most innovative advocates of the forward pass, made the following very strong statement about the importance of the run: "I've always thought there are two keys to winning in the NFL: being able to control the ball with your running game in the fourth quarter while disrupting the other team's offense with a dominating pass rush."[1]

---

1. Bill Walsh with Glenn Dickey. *Building a Champion: On Football and the Making of the 49ers*. (New York: St. Martin's Press, 1990). p. 141.

2

Tight Bunch Formations and Their Strategic Considerations

Balanced Variations of Tight Bunch

This book will present three variations of a balanced (doubles) bunch. These variations are illustrated in Diagrams 2-1a through 2-1c.

For the purpose of this book, the two receivers aligned on the line of scrimmage will be referred to as ends. The receiver aligned off the line toward the left side of the formation will be referred to as the slotback, and the receiver aligned off the line toward the right side of the formation will be referred to as the wingback. The lone running back will be referred to as the aceback. The type of run/pass plays that a coach intends to emphasize will determine what type of personnel will be utilized at the four receiver positions. These four players will probably be a mixture of tight ends, running backs, and/or wide receivers.

The primary advantage of both the balanced and unbalanced variations of bunch is that they force the defense to defend 10 gaps and cover four pass receivers who are aligned on, or near, the line of scrimmage. The following are some strategic considerations regarding defensive adjustments to the balanced variations of bunch:

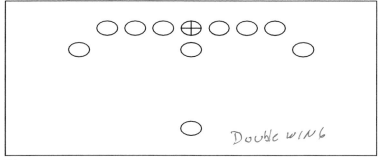

Diagram 2-1a

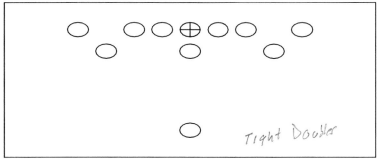

Diagram 2-1b

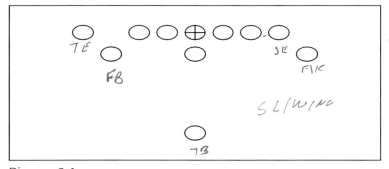

Diagram 2-1c

- A seven-man defensive front playing a variation of cover 2 will only be able to defend nine gaps. The defense will probably attempt to compensate for this by assigning one defender two gaps. This adjustment may cause the defense to have difficulty covering four vertical pass routes by the four receivers aligned on the line of scrimmage.

- A seven-man defensive front playing a rover secondary will only be able to defend eight gaps. This variation will probably be vulnerable toward the side of the defense away from the rover. Occasionally, this variation will attempt to maintain containment with their outside linebacker away from the rover and render itself extremely vulnerable to the off-tackle play (Diagram 2-2).

- An eight-man defensive front will only be able to defend eight gaps. This defensive variation will probably be vulnerable in the D gap. Occasionally, an eight-man front will move its ends to a 9 technique and assign them D-gap responsibility and leave them vulnerable in the C gap (Diagram 2-3).

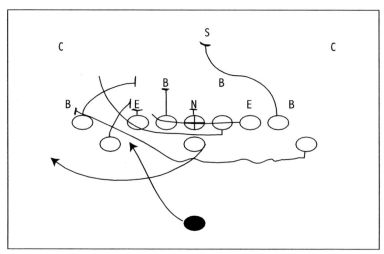

Diagram 2-2

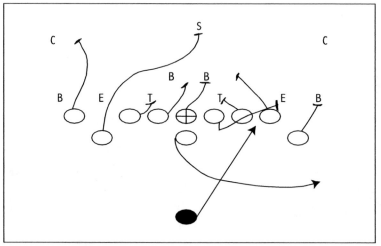

Diagram 2-3

Unbalanced Variations of Tight Bunch

Diagrams 2-4a through 2-4e illustrate five unbalanced (trips) variations of the tight bunch.

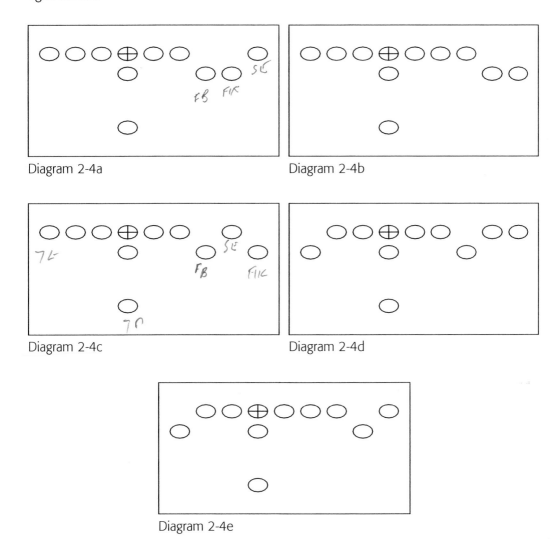

Diagram 2-4a

Diagram 2-4b

Diagram 2-4c

Diagram 2-4d

Diagram 2-4e

The unbalanced variations of bunch force the defense to defend six gaps toward the bunch and four gaps away from it. The following are some strategic considerations regarding defensive adjustments to the unbalanced variations of bunch:

- If a seven-man defensive front attempts to play a balanced variation of cover 2 (one cornerback on each side of the formation), it will leave one gap toward the bunch side of the formation unprotected (usually the E gap).

- If a seven-man defensive front plays a corner-over variation of cover 2, it will have a containment problem away from the bunch. This problem will be enhanced by quick motion (Diagram 2-5).

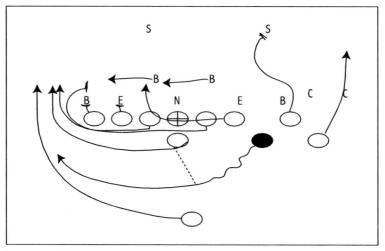

Diagram 2-5

- If a defensive front attempts to employ a rover secondary, they will only be able to defend eight gaps. They will therefore be vulnerable in one gap toward the bunch (usually the E gap) and have a containment problem away from the rover (which can also be enhanced by quick motion).

- An eight-man defensive front is in serious trouble versus an unbalanced variation of bunch. If the eight-man front remains balanced, it will leave two gaps toward the bunch unprotected (Diagram 2-6).

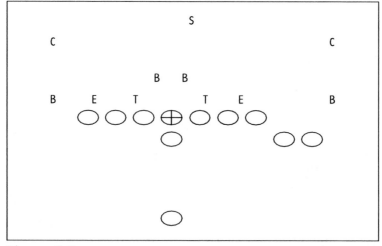

Diagram 2-6

- If, on the other hand, the eight-man front treats the bunch as an unbalanced line and has everyone move down a man toward the bunch, it will be weak in three areas. First, it will have a weakside containment problem (which can be enhanced by quick motion). Next, it will be vulnerable in one of the gaps toward the bunch (usually the E gap) and finally, all of the defenders will be aligned in unfamiliar positions reading different keys. Because the bunch formation forces the defense to defend 10 gaps, it is necessary to add two extra gaps to the universal letter system of gap designation (A, B, C, and D). The two additional gaps will be referred to as E and F (Diagram 2-7a and 2-7b).

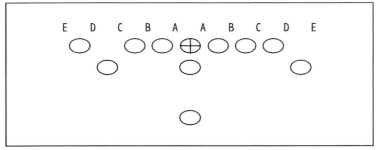

Diagram 2-7a

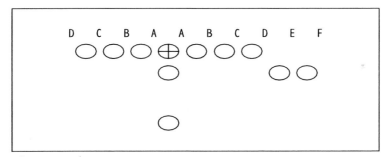

Diagram 2-7b

3

Installing a System of Comprehensive Blocking Assignments

Teaching an offensive lineman *who* to block is just as important as teaching him *how* to block. In this book, blocking assignments will be conveyed via rule blocking. Many coaches have abandoned rule blocking because of its complexity, but for almost two decades, rule blocking has enabled teams to enter each and every game knowing how to block virtually every defense in football. Nothing is sadder than seeing a team despondent in defeat because they were bewildered and frustrated by a surprise defense that they were not prepared to block.

Rule blocking conveys blocking assignments through the use of words such as gap, on, over, and so forth. These words depict the various alignments in which defenders may be positioned. Rule blocking assignments group words in order of priority. Players simply progress through the order of these words until they encounter a defender aligned in one of these positions. An offensive lineman who is assigned "gap, on, over," for example, will first check gap. If a defender is aligned in the gap, the lineman will block the gap defender. If no defender is in the gap, the lineman will then check on. If a defender is aligned in the on position, the lineman will block him. If no defender is in the on position, the lineman will then block the defender over him. Rule blocking requires that linemen both memorize their word priority assignments for each play, and know the specific defensive alignment represented by each word.

Rule Blocking Terms

Following are the words (arranged in priority) that are used to designate defensive alignments in the rule blocking system.

Attackside and Backside

Attackside refers to the side of the line in which the play is being run. *Backside* refers to the side of the line away from the point of attack. If the play is being run to the right, the right guard and tackle are both attackside linemen and will follow attackside blocking rules. The left guard and left tackle are backside linemen and will follow backside blocking rules. The center is neither backside nor attackside and will thus only have one blocking rule for each play.

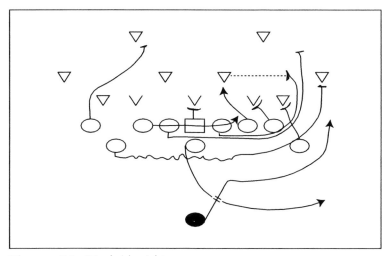

Diagram 3-1. Attackside right

Gap

Gap refers to any defensive lineman aligned between two offensive linemen. When a guard or tackle is assigned to block gap, he will always block toward the ball. When the center is assigned to block gap, he will always block the attackside gap (Diagram 3-2).

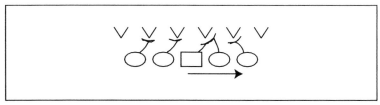

Diagram 3-2. Gap

Gap also refers to any defensive lineman playing inside shade on an offensive lineman (Diagram 3-3). In a split defense, the four defenders aligned inside of the tackles are considered aligned in the gaps (Diagrams 3-4 and 3-5).

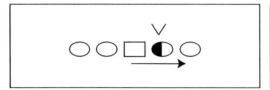

Diagram 3-3. Gap

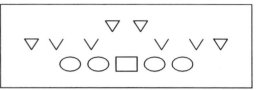

Diagram 3-4. Block the split as though the alignment was identical to Diagram 3-5.

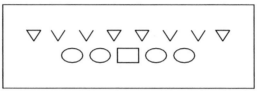

Diagram 3-5.

On

A defensive player is *on* when he is playing on the line of scrimmage and aligned head up (Diagram 3-6) or outside shade (Diagram 3-7) of an offensive lineman.

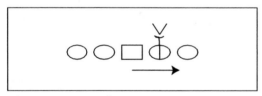

Diagram 3-6. Head up

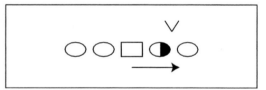

Diagram 3-7. Outside shade

Over

Over refers to a linebacker who is playing in front of an offensive lineman (Diagram 3-8).

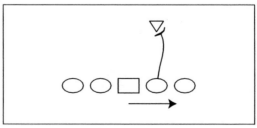

Diagram 3-8. Over

Inside

Inside refers to a defensive lineman who is aligned in the gap (Diagram 3-9), or on the next offensive lineman to the inside (Diagram 3-10).

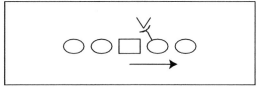 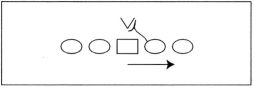

Diagram 3-9. Inside   Diagram 3-10. Inside

Outside

Outside is the exact opposite of inside. (Diagrams 3-11 and 3-12).

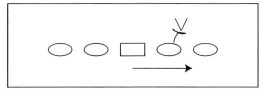 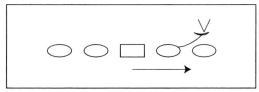

Diagram 3-11. Outside   Diagram 3-12. Outside

Linebacker

Linebacker refers to the most dangerous linebacker away from the point of attack. Thus, if the attackside is right and a lineman is assigned to block linebacker, he will block the most dangerous linebacker to his left (Diagram 3-13).

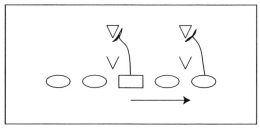

Diagram 3-13. Linebacker

Fill

Fill tells the backside tackle to block any defender aligned in his inside gap (Diagram 3-14), or pull and lead through the attackside B gap (Diagram 3-15).

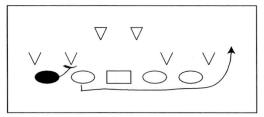

Diagram 3-14. Fill

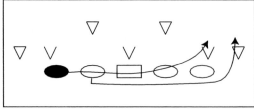

Diagram 3-15. Fill

Backside Gap

Backside is a pass blocking assignment; it instructs a lineman to block any defender aligned in the gap away from the direction of the play (Diagrams 3-16a and 3-16b).

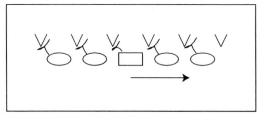

Diagram 3-16a. Backside gap versus gap

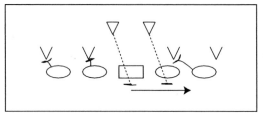

Diagram 3-16b. Backside gap versus split

Hunt

Hunt is also a pass blocking assignment; it instructs a lineman to block the most dangerous linebacker in his area (Diagram 3-17a and 3-17b).

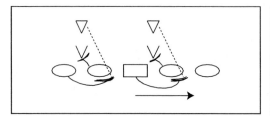

Diagram 3-17a. Hunt

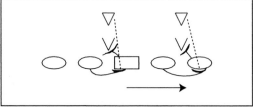

Diagram 3-17b. Hunt

Away

This assignment is for the center only. *Away* instructs him to block the most dangerous defender backside. Diagrams 3-18a through 3-18d illustrate four examples of away.

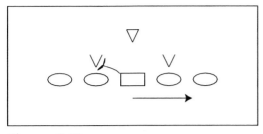

Diagram 3-18a

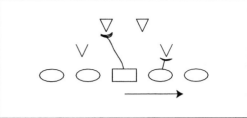

Diagram 3-18b

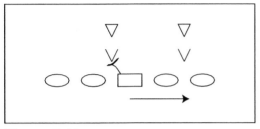

Diagram 3-18c

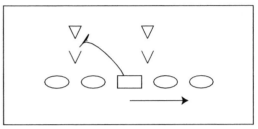

Diagram 3-18d

Reach

This assignment is for the attackside guard only. *Reach* instructs him to block a defensive lineman in the B gap (Diagram 3-19).

Tandem

This assignment is for the attackside tackle. *Tandem* instructs him to block the stacked linebacker in a 5-3 stack defense (Diagram 3-20).

Stack

Stack refers to a linebacker stacked behind the 0 technique (Diagram 3-21).

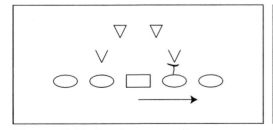

Diagram 3-19. Reach versus split

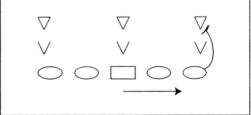

Diagram 3-20. Tandem

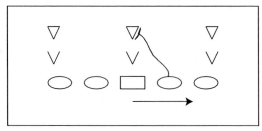

Diagram 3-21. Stack

Fold

Fold may be assigned when the AST is not covered by a defensive lineman, and the ASG has a defender playing on him, or in his outside gap (Diagrams 3-22a and 3-22b).

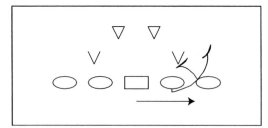

Diagram 3-22a. Fold versus split   Diagram 3-22b. Fold versus college

Rule

A lineman assigned *rule* will follow this progression: "gap, on, over, linebacker."

Numbering

When numbers are used to convey blocking assignments, number the defenders in the defensive front from the outside in. Diagrams 3-23a and 3-23b illustrate how to number both the 5-2 and split defenses.

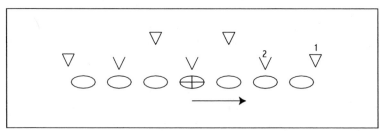

Diagram 3-23a. Numbering the 5-2

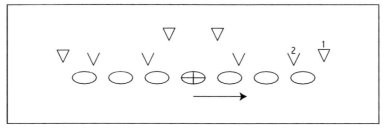

Diagram 3-23b. Numbering the split defense

Him blocking

Him blocking means that the blocking assignment cannot be put into words or numbers; it is therefore based upon defensive recognition. In other words, each lineman must know which "him" to block.

4

Sequence

To my way of thinking it is a great mistake to try to pick individual plays from various sound systems of offense and group them together to form an attack. When this is done there is no real sequence of plays and since the true value in any attack is its ability to look the same and still strike at different areas in the defense the sound concept and thorough exploitation of a real system is of vital importance.[1]

—Bud Wilkinson

Over the years I have always held in high regard the explosiveness of the basic concept of sequence football. I have seen properly sequenced plays storm the castle, but this was not so much the result of strategy as the natural impulse of the defense. When plays look or start out like previously run successful plays, a team reacts to past knowledge. Some of these plays may not even employ the most advantageous style of blocking, but the large factors of deception and sequence make them successful.[2]

—Ara Parseghian

Read any old football book written by one of the masters of the run offense and somewhere there will be some mention of sequence. The difference between a bunch of plays and a real offensive—as it pertains to the running game—is sequence. Sequence can be defined as the grouping of similar backfield actions for the purpose of:

- Attacking the defense over a broad front. A sequential series will attack all sectors of the defense—the inside sector, the off-tackle hole, the perimeter, and the secondary.

- Causing uncertainty in the minds of defensive players. A sequential play that strikes the inside sector of the defense will have the same initial appearance as one of its counterparts that attacks the off-tackle hole, the perimeter, and the secondary. Therefore, as a play begins, the defenders are initially uncertain as to the exact area of the defense that the play is attacking.

- Placing defenders in assignment conflict dilemmas. This tactic is referred to as *double-binding* a player. For example, if the offensive tackle blocks inside, a defender playing a 5 technique will be vulnerable to the trap if he does not close inside. On the other hand, if he does close inside, he will be vulnerable to an off-tackle play, or sweep, if the tight end crack blocks him. So what should he do?

Sequence inhibits defensive play recognition, slows defensive pursuit, destroys defensive keys and confidence, and ultimately, abates defensive aggression. Every play in this book will be organized into a sequential series.

1. Charles "Bud" Wilkinson. *Oklahoma Split T Football*. (New York: Prentice-Hall, 1952). p. 241.

2. Ara Parseghian and Tom Pagna. *Parseghian and Notre Dame Football*. (Garden City, NY: Doubleday, 1973). p. 228.

5

The Power Series

The power series is one of the oldest and most explosive series in football. It has two specific features: first, the aceback off-tackle play is the leadoff play and every play in the series begins with this threat; and second, the slotback will go into motion toward the attack side and serve as a lead blocker.

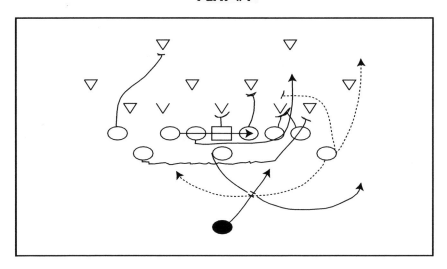

DESCRIPTION & BLOCKING RULES: Off-tackle power. **Power blocking rules.**

COACHING POINTS: This play is the leadoff play of the series. It is a trademark play that the offense must be able to run any place under any conditions. If the defense is ever able to stop the off-tackle power, it is because it has *cheated* and left itself vulnerable to another play in the series. Note that the wingback may do one of three things: one, influence #1 and seal inside; two, release downfield and fake a pass pattern; or three, fake counter action. These three options should be incorporated into a sideline call and not left to the wingback's discretion. All three options set up other plays in the series.

ASE: Blocks #2

AST: Rule

ASG: Rule

C: On, away

BSG: Pull and lead

BST: Fill

BSE: Downfield

QB: Reverse pivots and deals the ball to the aceback as deep as possible. Fakes the quarterback keep. Does not look at the aceback after handing the ball off; instead, "eyeballs" the defender responsible for primary run support to determine if he will cover if the quarterback keeps the ball.

ACE: Steps directly at the hole. Does not look for the ball; it is the quarterback's responsibility to get it to him. Protects the ball with both hands until he is out of traffic. Runs to daylight.

SB: Goes into motion and kicks out #1. Blocks #1 at the hip with his right shoulder.

WB: Executes the option called in the huddle.

PLAY #2

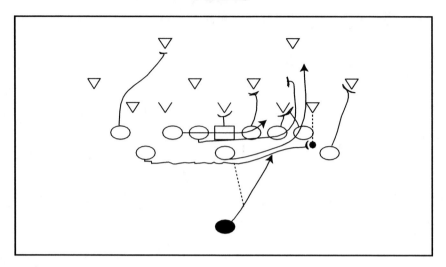

DESCRIPTION & BLOCKING RULES: Off-tackle power pitch. **Power blocking rules.**

COACHING POINTS: This method is an alternative approach toward running the play. When this method is chosen, the wingback will block the defender responsible for primary run support.

ASE: Blocks #2

AST: Rule

ASG: Rule

C: On, away

BSG: Pull and lead

BST: Fill

BSE: Downfield

QB: Steps laterally with his right foot. Gains depth as he makes this step. As his right foot makes contact with the ground, he pivots on it and softly tosses the ball to the aceback. Leads the play through the off-tackle hole. As he leads, he will be shoulder-to-shoulder with the pulling guard.

ACE: Takes a slight lateral jab step before aiming directly toward the hole. Locks the ball into his hands and immediately secures it. Protects the ball with both hands while in traffic.

SB: Goes into motion and kicks out #1. Blocks him at the hip with his right shoulder.

WB: Blocks the defender responsible for primary run support.

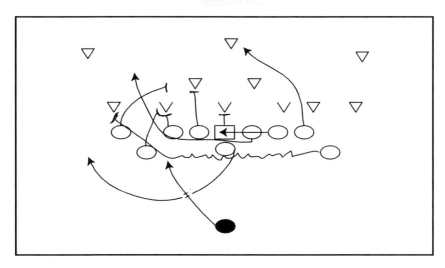

DESCRIPTION & BLOCKING RULES: Off-tackle power toward the slotback. **Power blocking rules.**

COACHING POINTS: Occasionally, a team will leave a huge void toward the slot side of the formation by playing #1 outside of the tight end (a defense employing a cover 3 rover will often do this). When this occurs, the defense gives the offense great angles and the off-tackle power should be a big gainer.

ASE: Seals the second level inside.

AST: Rule

ASG: Rule

C: On, away

BSG: Pull and lead

BST: Fills

BSE: Downfield

QB: Reverse pivots and deals the ball to the aceback as deep as possible. Fakes the quarterback keep. Does not look at the aceback after he hands the ball off; instead, "eyeballs" the defender responsible for primary run support to determine if the defender will cover the quarterback if he keeps the ball.

ACE: Steps directly at the hole. Does not look for the ball; it is the quarterback's responsibility to get it to him. Protects the ball with both hands until he is out of traffic. Runs to daylight.

SB: Blocks #2

WB: Goes into motion and kicks out #1. Blocks him at the hip with his left shoulder.

Bounce

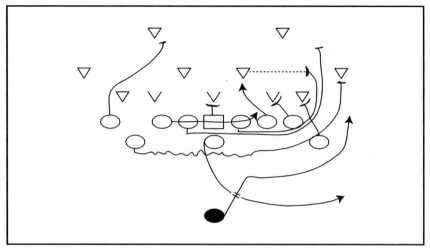

DESCRIPTION & BLOCKING RULES: This play is an aceback bounce that gives the initial impression that an off-tackle power is in progress. **Bounce blocking rules.**

COACHING POINTS: One variation of Play #1 features a tactic in which the wingback pretends to crack block #1 and then seals inside. In this play, the wingback actually crack blocks #1. These two tactics double-bind #1. If #1 ignores the wingback's influence in Play #1 and closes inside to stop the off-tackle power, he is vulnerable to this play, and vice versa.

ASE: Inside, linebacker

AST: Inside, linebacker

ASG: Pulls and leads, looks for the inside linebacker.

C: Gap, on, away

BSG: Gap, pull and lead

BST: Fills

BSE: Downfield

QB: Reverse pivots and deals the ball to the aceback as deep as possible, and then fakes the quarterback keep.

ACE: His first step is a crossover step with his left foot. Next, he steps with his right foot and then the left. He will have possession of the ball by the time he makes his third step. Plants on his third step and breaks the play outside. Runs to daylight.

SB: Goes into motion and blocks the defensive back responsible for primary run support. If this defender comes to the line of scrimmage quickly, he kicks him out (attacks defender's inside hip with his right shoulder). If defender plays soft, he runs over him (attacks defender's outside hip with his left shoulder).

WB: Blocks #1. Caves him inside.

Bounce

PLAY #5

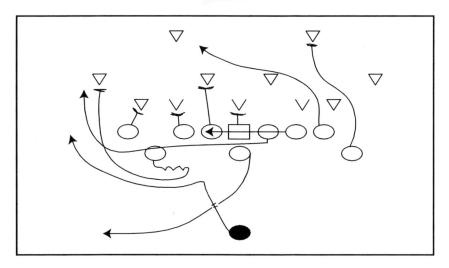

DESCRIPTION & BLOCKING RULES: This aceback bounce is a variation of Play #4. **Weakside power blocking rules.**

COACHING POINTS: When #1 remains inside of the tight end when the slotback goes into motion, he is vulnerable to the tight end's crack block.

ASE: Inside, linebacker

AST: Rule

ASG: Rule

C: On, away

BSG: Pull and lead

BST: Fill

BSE: Downfield

QB: Reverse pivots and deals the ball to the aceback as deep as possible, and then fakes the quarterback keep.

ACE: His first step is a crossover step with his right foot. Next, he steps with his left foot and then the right. He will have possession of the ball by the time he makes his third step. Plants on his third step and breaks the play outside. Runs to daylight.

SB: Goes into reverse motion and blocks the first defender outside of the ASE's block.

WB: Downfield

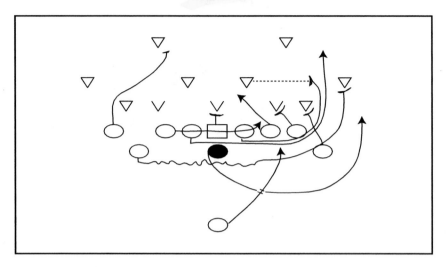

DESCRIPTION & BLOCKING RULES: This quarterback keep utilizes sweep blocking principles. **Bounce blocking rules.**

COACHING POINTS: This play is great for a quarterback who likes to run the ball. It should be called when the secondary defender responsible for primary run support ignores the quarterback's fake or is playing soft.

ASE: Inside, linebacker

AST: Inside, linebacker

ASG: Pulls and leads, looks for the inside linebacker.

C: Gap, on, away

BSG: Gap, pull and lead

BST: Fill

BSE: Downfield

QB: Reverse pivots and makes a great fake to the aceback. Flashes the ball at the aceback with both hands and then quickly hides it on his right hip with his right hand as he simultaneously rides the aceback with his left hand. Hides the ball on his hip for as long as possible. Looking at the aceback after he fakes to him will enhance the effectiveness of his fake.

ACE: Fakes off-tackle power. Makes a great fake by slapping his left elbow with his right hand and then running toward the off-tackle hole with great intensity.

SB: Goes into motion and blocks the defensive back responsible for primary run support.

WB: Blocks #1, caves him inside.

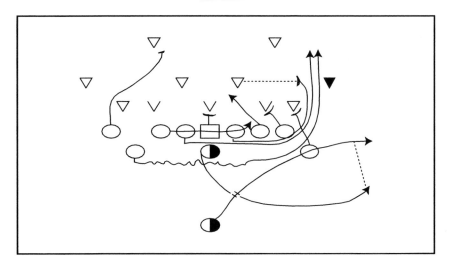

DESCRIPTION & BLOCKING RULES: The quarterback will keep the ball after faking to the aceback, and then have the option of executing a shovel pass back to the aceback or keeping the ball. **Bounce blocking rules.**

COACHING POINTS: The defender responsible for primary run support will be left unblocked. The quarterback will read this defender and either keep the ball or shovel pass it to the aceback. This play is especially effective versus overly aggressive cover 2 cornerbacks.

ASE: Inside, linebacker

AST: Inside, linebacker

ASG: Pulls and leads, looks for the inside linebacker.

C: Gap, on, away

BSG: Gap, pull and lead

BST: Fill

BSE: Downfield

QB: Fakes the ball to the aceback. As he is attacking the perimeter, reads the defensive back responsible for primary run support. If defensive back plays him aggressively, quickly executes a shovel pass to the tailback.

ACE: Steps exactly as he did when he bounced the off-tackle play outside. Aims his course directly at the defensive back responsible for primary run support, but makes sure that his path does not cross the line of scrimmage and cause a penalty (lineman downfield on a forward pass). If the DB being optioned plays soft and/or covers him, block the DB.

SB: Goes into motion and blocks safety.

WB: Blocks #1, caves him inside.

PLAY #8

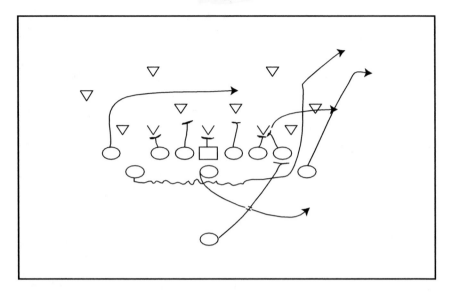

DESCRIPTION & BLOCKING RULES: This play-action pass is set up by successful execution of the off-tackle power. **Standard pass pro blocking rules**.

COACHING POINTS: This flood route high-lows the flats.

ASE: Blocks inside for three counts and then releases on a shallow delay route (three to five yards) into the flats.

AST: On, backside gap, hunt

ASG: On, backside gap, hunt

C: On, backside gap, hunt

BSG: On, backside gap, hunt

BST: On, backside gap, hunt

BSE: Finds windows as he drags across the formation at a depth of three to seven yards.

QB: Fakes the off-tackle power and continue to roll into the flats. Reads the cornerback.

ACE: Fakes the off-tackle power and then blocks #1.

SB: Goes into motion and runs a flag route.

WB: Releases immediately as the ball is snapped and runs an 18-yard out pattern.

Throw Back

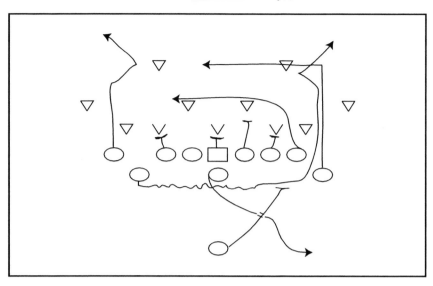

DESCRIPTION & BLOCKING RULES: Like the previous play, this play-action pass is also set up by successful execution of the off-tackle power. **Standard pass pro blocking rules.**

COACHING POINTS: This pass high-lows the hook zones away from the run fake.

ASE: Runs a five-to-six-yard drag across the formation.

AST: On, backside gap, hunt

ASG: On, backside gap, hunt

C: On, backside gap, hunt

BSG: On, backside gap, hunt

BST: On, backside gap, hunt

BSE: Runs a post-corner route.

QB: Fakes the off-tackle power, sets deep, and reads the reactions of the inside linebackers.

ACE: Fakes the off-tackle power and then blocks #1.

SB: Goes into motion and runs a post-corner route.

WB: Releases immediately as the ball is snapped and runs an 18-yard square in pattern.

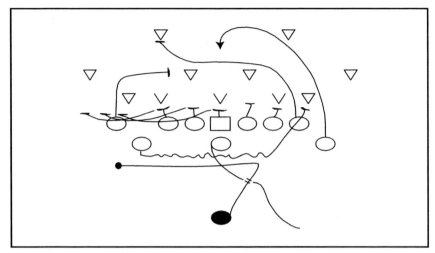

DESCRIPTION & BLOCKING RULES: This screen exploits defenses that pursue carelessly from the backside. **Standard pass pro blocking rules.**

COACHING POINTS: The line will follow their normal pass pro blocking rules for three counts and then release to their designated screen areas. It is vital that the offensive linemen hold their initial blocks for three counts and then do a great acting job that fools defenders into believing that their pass rush techniques have been successful.

ASE: Downfield

AST: On, backside gap, hunt

ASG: On, backside gap, hunt

C: Blocks on, backside gap, hunts for three counts, and releases to his designated screen area.

BSG: Blocks on, backside gap, hunts for three counts, and releases to his designated screen area.

BST: Blocks on, backside gap, hunts for three counts, and releases to his designated screen area.

BSE: Releases outside and seals off inside linebacker pursuit.

QB: Fakes the off-tackle power, sets deep, and delivers the ball to either the tailback or wingback (the wingback is his outlet if the defense successfully reads screen).

ACE: Fakes the off-tackle power. Aceback should make a great fake and get to his designated screen area.

SB: Goes into motion and blocks #1.

WB: Releases inside at a depth of 10 yards, and finds a window between the tackles. He is the quarterback's outlet.

PLAY #11

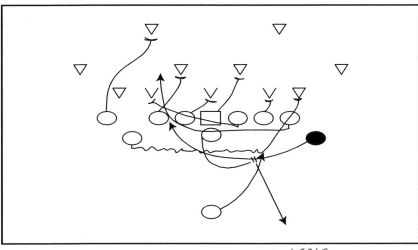

WINGTRIP

DESCRIPTION & BLOCKING RULES: This quick hitting counter exploits swift defensive pursuit. **Counter blocking rules.**

COACHING POINTS: This play has a high potential for a fumble. As a result, the execution of the quarterback and the wingback must be meticulous.

ASE: Downfield

AST: If the attackside guard is covered, blocks on, over, outside. If the attackside guard is uncovered, blocks linebacker.

ASG: Inside, linebacker (exception: split-4)

C: Away (exception: split-4)

BSG: Pull and trap

BST: On, over, outside

BSE: Pull and lead

QB: Reverse pivots and quickly seats the ball (seat: bring the ball to his belt buckle). His reverse pivot will be as deep as the off-tackle power. Locks the ball into the wingback's pouch as he hands off. Does not fake to the aceback after the handoff. Instead, drops back as though he intends to pass.

ACE: Fakes the off-tackle power.

SB: Goes motion and blocks #1. The path of his motion must not hinder the tight end's pull.

WB: Gains depth on his first step. Makes a good pouch. Secures the ball and protects it while in traffic. Runs to daylight.

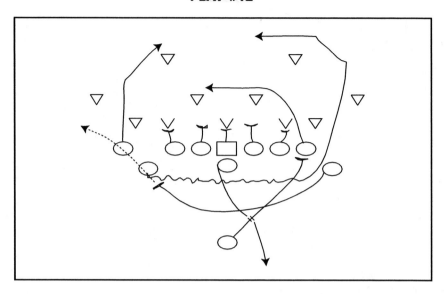

DESCRIPTION & BLOCKING RULES: This play-action pass features misdirection and exploits the area of the pass defense away from the off-tackle fake. **Standard pass pro blocking rules.**

COACHING POINTS: This pass high-lows the hook zones.

ASE: Releases inside and runs a five-yard drag across the formation.

AST: On, backside gap, hunt

ASG: On, backside gap, hunt

C: On, backside gap, hunt

BSG: On, backside gap, hunt

BST: On, backside gap, hunt

BSE: Runs a post route.

QB: Fakes the off-tackle power, hides the ball on his right hip and then sets deep. Reads the drop of the inside linebackers.

ACE: Fakes the off-tackle power and then blocks #1.

SB: Goes into motion and runs a dig route.

WB: Fakes the counter and blocks #1 backside. If #1 drops into coverage, releases shallow into the flats.

PLAY #13

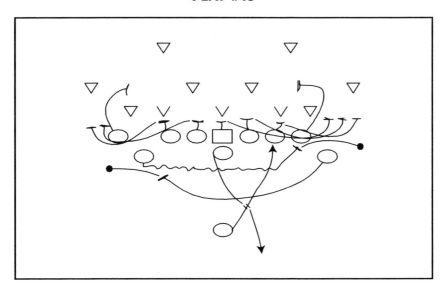

DESCRIPTION & BLOCKING RULES: This double-screen fakes the counter and provides the offense with excellent misdirection. **Standard pass pro blocking rules.**

COACHING POINTS: The line will follow their normal pass pro blocking rules for three counts and then release to their designated screen areas (attackside is right).

ASE: Releases outside and seals off the inside linebacker.

AST: First, blocks on, backside gap, hunt, and releases to his designated screen area.

ASG: First, blocks on, backside gap, hunt, and releases to his designated screen area.

C: First, blocks on, backside gap, hunt, and releases to his designated screen area.

BSG: First, blocks on, backside gap, hunt, and releases to his designated screen area.

BST: First, blocks on, backside gap, hunt, and releases to his designated screen area.

BSE: Releases outside and seals off the inside linebacker.

QB: Fakes the counter, sets deep, reads the inside linebackers, and dumps the ball off to the wingback or slotback.

ACE: Fakes the off-tackle power.

SB: Goes into motion and blocks #1, and releases for his screen route.

WB: Fakes the counter, blocks #1, and releases for his screen route.

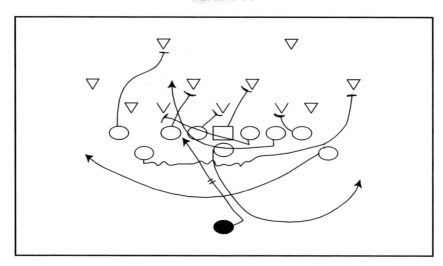

DESCRIPTION & BLOCKING RULES: The blocking and backfield action is what most coaches call the counter trey. **Otis blocking rules.**

COACHING POINTS: The addition of the wingback and quarterback action enhances the play's intended misdirection and leads to a number of significant complementary plays.

ASE: Downfield

AST: If the guard is covered, blocks on, over, outside. If the guard is uncovered, blocks linebacker.

ASG: Inside, linebacker (exception: split-4)

C: Away (exception: split-4)

BSG: Pull and trap

BST: Pull and lead

BSE: Fills inside.

QB: Reverses slightly deeper than he would for the off-tackle power. Deals the ball to the aceback and fakes the naked boot. Eyeballs #1 (backside defender) to make certain that #1 is covering him.

ACE: Makes his first step a crossover step with his left foot. His next step will be with his right foot. Plants on this step, receives the ball, and runs to daylight. Keys the block of the backside tackle as he approaches the line of scrimmage.

SB: Goes into motion and blocks the defensive back responsible for primary run support.

WB: Fakes the reverse by making a good pouch and slaps his right elbow with his left hand as he passes the quarterback.

PLAY #15

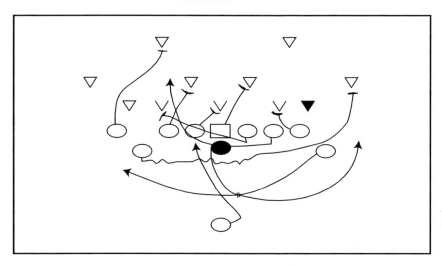

NAKED Boot off MD

DESCRIPTION & BLOCKING RULES: Naked boot. This play is exactly the same as the previous play with one exception: the quarterback will fake the ball to the aceback and keep it. **Otis blocking rules** (opposite direction of the play).

COACHING POINTS: The offense is leaving the #1 attackside defender unblocked, Therefore, the naked boot should only be called when #1 does not guard the quarterback. This can be ascertained by the quarterback's observation and/or determined by the eye in the sky

ASE: Fills inside.

AST: Pull and lead

ASG: Pull and trap

C: Away (exception: split-4)

BSG: Inside, linebacker (exception: split-4)

BST: If the guard is covered, blocks on, over, outside. If the guard is uncovered, blocks linebacker.

BSE: Downfield

QB: Reverse pivots as he did on the counter trey. Seats the ball and hides it from the defense. Fakes the ball to the wingback, puts the ball on his right hip, and runs the naked boot to daylight.

ACE: Fakes the counter trey by making a good pouch and slapping his right elbow with his left hand as he passes the imaginary mesh point.

SB: Goes into motion and blocks the defensive back responsible for primary run support.

WB: Fakes the reverse by making a good pouch and slaps his right elbow with his left hand as he passes the quarterback.

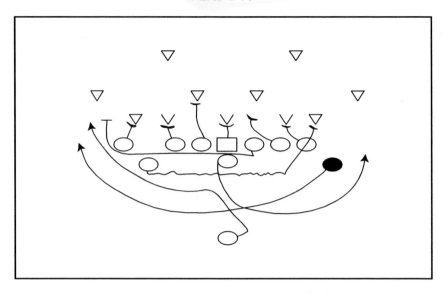

DESCRIPTION & BLOCKING RULES: This play is a reverse. **Variation of weakside power blocking rules.**

COACHING POINTS: This play is best used early in the game. A fast wingback is required to run the play well.

ASE: Blocks #1

AST: On, over, outside

ASG: On, over, reach, tandem, linebacker

C: Gap, on, away

BSG: Gap, pull and lead

BST: Fills inside.

BSE: Fills inside.

QB: Reverse pivots as he did for the counter trey and hands the ball to the wingback. He does not need to fake to the aceback. After the handoff, he fakes the naked boot.

ACE: Fakes the counter trey. After he passes the quarterback, plants on his right foot and leads the play to the perimeter.

SB: Goes into motion and blocks #1.

WB: Receives the ball from the quarterback and gets around end as quickly as possible.

WING POWER

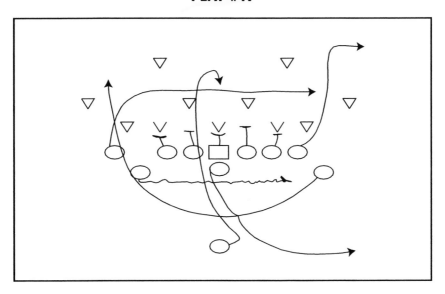

DESCRIPTION & BLOCKING RULES: Counter trey pass. **Standard pass pro blocking rules.**

COACHING POINTS: This play-action pass features excellent misdirection, creates a high low of the flats, and has good throwback potential.

ASE: Releases outside and runs a 15-yard out.

AST: On, backside gap, hunt

ASG: On, backside gap, hunt

C: On, backside gap, hunt

ASG: On, backside gap, hunt

AST: On, backside gap, hunt

ASE: Runs a five-yard drag across the formation.

QB: Fakes the counter trey, rolls right, and reads the cornerback.

ACE: Fakes the counter trey and then finds a window five yards between the two inside linebackers.

SB: Goes into motion and blocks #1.

WB: Fakes the reverse and streaks up the field.

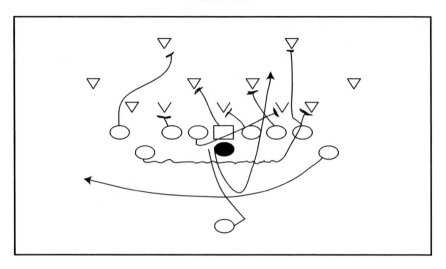

DESCRIPTION & BLOCKING RULES: This play is a quarterback trap. Its roots go all the way back to the single wing spinner series. **Him trap blocking rules.**

COACHING POINTS: Obviously, this play requires a tough, hard-nosed quarterback.

ASE: Him

AST: Him

ASG: Him

C: Him

BSG: Him

BST: Him

BSE: Him

QB: Reverse pivots at five o'clock. Plants on his second step, and reverses his direction toward the line of scrimmage. Reads the blocking and protects the ball in traffic.

ACE: Fakes the counter trey.

SB: Goes into motion and blocks #1.

WB: Fakes the reverse.

PLAY #19

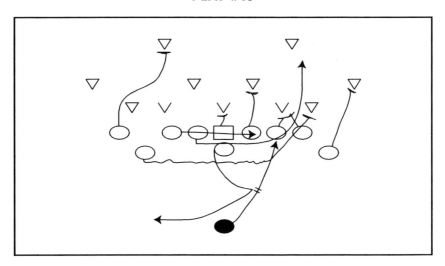

DESCRIPTION & BLOCKING RULES: This variation of the off-tackle power is enhanced by the quarterback's bootleg action and the wingback's downfield release. **Power blocking rules.**

COACHING POINTS: This play pressures the secondary by confusing its run/pass key. It also sets up the bootleg run and pass.

ASE: Blocks #2

AST: Rule

ASG: Rule

C: On, away

BSG: Pull and lead

BST: Fill

BSE: Downfield

QB: Reverse pivots and deals the ball to the aceback as deep as possible. After the handoff, fakes the bootleg.

ACE: Steps directly at the hole. Does not look for the ball; it is the quarterback's responsibility to get it to him. Protects the ball with both hands until he is out of traffic. Runs to daylight.

SB: Goes into motion and kicks out #1. Blocks him at the hip with his right shoulder.

WB: Blocks the defensive back responsible for primary run support.

PLAY #20

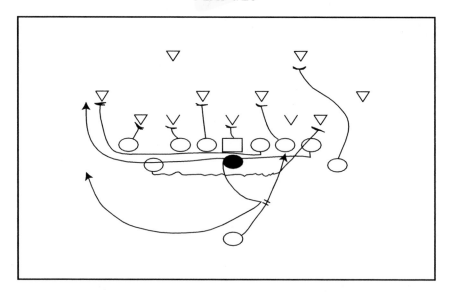

DESCRIPTION & BLOCKING RULES: This play is a predetermined quarterback bootleg run. **Punch blocking rules.**

COACHING POINTS: Many teams use this play in short yardage and goal line situations. It requires a tough mobile quarterback.

ASE: Blocks #1

AST: On, over, outside

ASG: On, over, reach, tandem, linebacker

C: Gap, on, away

BSG: Gap, pull and lead

BST: Fills inside.

BSE: Pull and lead

QB: Reverse pivots and fakes the off-tackle run. After the fake, hides the ball on his left hip and runs the bootleg. His fake to the aceback is the key element to the play's success.

ACE: Fakes the off-tackle power.

SB: Goes into motion and blocks #1.

WB: Downfield

PLAY #21

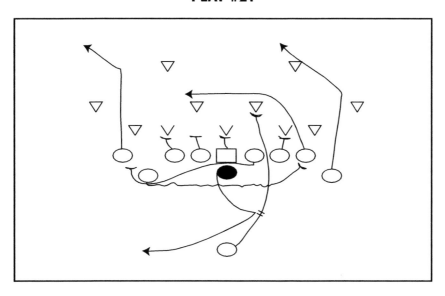

DESCRIPTION & BLOCKING RULES: This play-action pass features misdirection and exploits the area of the pass defense away from the off-tackle fake. **Bootleg pass blocking rules**.

COACHING POINTS: This pass high-lows the hook zones (attackside is left).

ASE: Runs a flag pattern

AST: On, backside gap, hunt

ASG: On, backside gap, hunt

C: On, away

BSG: Pulls playside and blocks tandem, #1.

BST: Rule

BSE: Releases inside and runs a five-yard drag across the formation.

QB: Fakes the off-tackle power, hides the ball on his left hip and bootlegs left. Reads the drop of the inside linebackers.

ACE: Fakes the off-tackle power and then fills for the pulling guard.

SB: Goes into motion and blocks #1.

WB: Runs a post route versus cover 2, and a dig versus everything else.

PLAY #22

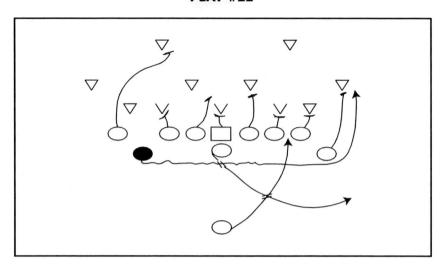

DESCRIPTION & BLOCKING RULES: This play forces the defense to pay cautious attention to slotback motion because it attacks the perimeter very quickly. **Base blocking rules.**

COACHING POINTS: The keys to success for this play are slotback speed and solid blocking from the wingback and tight end.

ASE: Blocks #1

AST: On, over, outside

ASG: On, over, reach, tandem, linebacker

C: Rule

BSG: Rule

BST: Rule

BSE: Downfield

QB: Reverse pivots at 180 degrees and quickly deals the ball to the slotback. After the handoff, fakes the off-tackle power.

ACE: Fakes off-tackle power.

SB: Goes into quick motion. Receives the handoff about a yard deeper than the quarterback. Runs to daylight.

WB: Blocks the defensive back responsible for primary run support.

6

The Slant Series

T he slant series is very similar to the power series because the lead off play is an aceback off-tackle play. The difference between the two series is that the slant series requires does not require a double-team at the point of attack, or a motion man to act as a lead blocker. Zone blocking rules could easily be substituted for slant blocking rules to engineer the series' lead off play, and the entire series could be renamed the zone series. Numerous discussions with college coaches, however, have led the author to believe that the inside zone is a very difficult play for most high schools to run efficiently. All of the plays in the slant series can be run from balanced formations, but many of the plays that will be illustrated will be done so from unbalanced formations. The purpose of this is to facilitate the discussion of defensive exploitation.

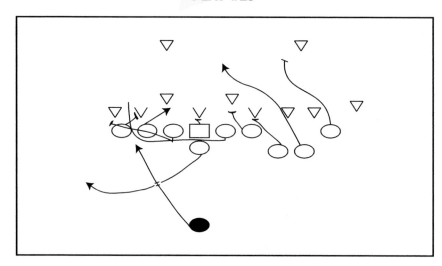

DESCRIPTION & BLOCKING RULES: This quick hitting slant play gives the offense great angles; it is the lead off play of the series. **Slant blocking rules.**

COACHING POINTS: The play is being illustrated away from the trips side of the formation because the defense is employing a corner-over secondary to match offensive strength. This leaves the safety responsible for primary weak side run support. If the safety fills too quickly however, the defense becomes vulnerable to the quarterback keep. (**Reminder:** this play can also be run employing base, punch, or zone blocking rules).

ASE: Blocks #2

AST: Inside, linebacker

ASG: Pulls and traps #1

C: Gap, on, away

BSG: Gap, pull and lead

BST: Fills if the guard pulls (listens for his call); otherwise, blocks rule.

BSE: Downfield

QB: Reverse pivots and deals the ball to the aceback as deep as possible. Fakes the quarterback keep. Does not look at the aceback after he hands the ball off; instead, "eyeballs" the DB responsible for primary run support to determine if he is respecting the keep.

ACE: Steps directly at the hole. Does not look for the ball; it is the quarterback's responsibility to get it to him. Protects the ball with both hands until he is out of traffic. Runs to daylight.

SB: Fills

WB: Downfield

PLAY #24

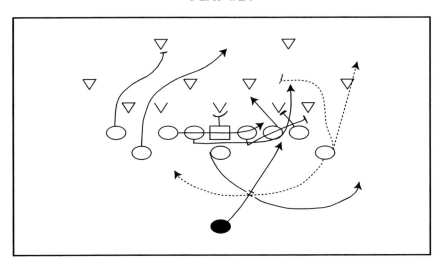

DESCRIPTION & BLOCKING RULES: This slant play is being run from a balanced formation. **Slant blocking rules.**

COACHING POINTS: When run from a balanced formation, the wingback can be given the same three options that he was given with the off-tackle power, and most of the sequential power plays can also be incorporated into this series. (**Reminder:** this play can also be run employing base, punch, or zone blocking rules).

ASE: Blocks #2

AST: Inside, linebacker

ASG: Pulls and traps #1

C: Gap, on, away

BSG: Gap, pull and lead

BST: Fills if the guard pulls (listens for his call), otherwise, blocks rule.

BSE: Downfield

QB: Reverse pivots and deals the ball to the aceback as deep as possible. Fakes the quarterback keep. Does not look at the aceback after he hands the ball off; instead, "eyeballs" the DB responsible for primary run support to determine if he is respecting the keep.

ACE: Steps directly at the hole. Does not look for the ball; it is the quarterback's responsibility to get it to him. Protects the ball with both hands until he is out of traffic. Runs to daylight.

SB: Downfield

WB: Same three options that were available to the off-tackle power play.

PLAY #25

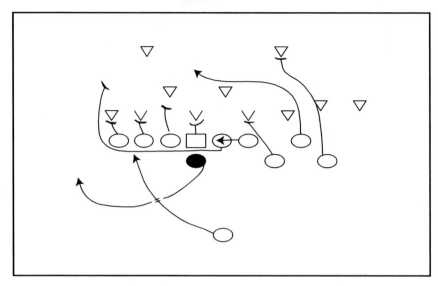

Belly Keep

DESCRIPTION & BLOCKING RULES: This play is the quarterback keep. **Punch blocking rules.**

COACHING POINTS: This play is being run away from the trips for the same reasons that Play 22 was. A coach can also have the quarterback give the ball to the aceback and have the aceback bounce the play outside or run off-tackle employing these blocking rules.

ASE: Blocks #1

AST: On, over, outside

ASG: On, over, reach, tandem, linebacker

C: Gap, on, away

BSG: Gap, pull and lead through the C gap

BST: Fill

BSE: Downfield

QB: Reverse pivots and fakes the ball to the aceback. Hides the ball on his left hip and reads the block of the pulling guard as he approaches the perimeter.

ACE: Fakes the off-tackle slant.

SB: Fills

WB: Downfield

PLAY #26

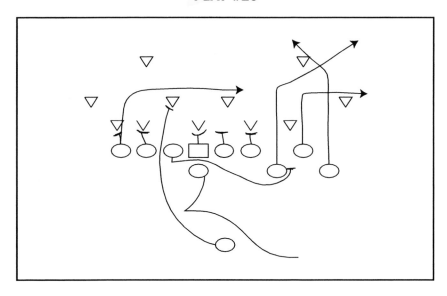

DESCRIPTION & BLOCKING RULES: Bootleg action can be incorporated into any of the slant variations. This play-action pass features misdirection and exploits the area of the pass defense away from the off-tackle fake. **Bootleg pass protection.**

COACHING POINTS: This pass high-lows the flats. It is an excellent play when a cover 2 secondary remains balanced versus trips (attackside is right).

ASE: Releases straight upfield and runs a 10-yard out pattern.

AST: On, backside gap, hunt

ASG: On, backside gap, hunt

C: On, away

BSG: Pulls playside and blocks tandem, #1

BST: Rule

BSE: Slams #1 and then runs a five-yard drag across the formation.

QB: Fakes the slant, hides the ball on his right hip and then rolls right. Reads the cornerback.

ACE: Fake the slant and then fills for the pulling guard.

SB: Runs a flag pattern.

WB: Runs a post pattern.

F-NGBelly
Boot

674

Key CB

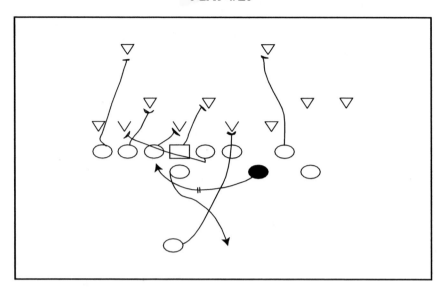

Belly
QB TRAP

DESCRIPTION & BLOCKING RULES: This extremely quick hitting counter employs counter trey blocking principles. **Otis blocking rules.**

COACHING POINTS: This play has a moderate risk of a ballhandling error if adequate practice time is not devoted to it.

ASE: Downfield

AST: If the guard is covered, blocks on, over, outside. If the guard is uncovered, blocks linebacker.

ASG: Inside, linebacker (exception: split-4)

C: Away (exception: split-4)

BSG: Pull and trap

BST: Pull and lead

BSE: Downfield

QB: First, takes a jab step straight back with his right foot; this will enable him to gain enough depth to allow the slotback a clear path to the hole. Makes sure to seat the ball securely as he takes this jab step. Next, pivots on his right foot so that his left foot is pointing at about 4 o'clock. Now, deals the ball to the slotback and then sets deep to simulate an intention to pass.

ACE: Fakes the slant and fills for the pulling tackle.

SB: Immediately gets to the mesh point and secures the ball as he bursts through traffic.

WB: Downfield

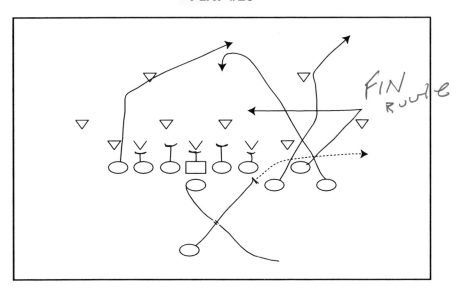

DESCRIPTION & BLOCKING RULES: This play-action pass creates some great rubs and is effective versus any type of secondary coverage. **Standard pass pro blocking rules.**

COACHING POINTS: This pattern exploits man coverage by creating natural picks. It isolates the frontside hook area versus any zone coverage. It also isolates the frontside free safety versus any variation of cover 2.

ASE: Runs a five-yard arrow and in pattern.

AST: On, backside gap, hunt

ASG: On, backside gap, hunt

C: On, backside gap, hunt

BSG: On, backside gap, hunt

BST: On, backside gap, hunt

BSE: Runs a post pattern.

QB: Fakes the slant and continues to roll deep into the flats. Reads the frontside linebacker (and free safety if cover 2 is employed).

ACE: Fakes the off-tackle power and then blocks #1. If #1 drops into coverage, runs a five-yard out.

SB: Creates a 3-4 yard rub with the wingback and then runs a post-corner pattern.

WB: Creates a 3-4 yard rub with the slotback and then finds an 18-yard window in the frontside hook zone.

PLAY #29

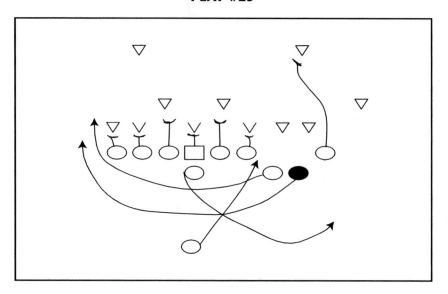

DESCRIPTION & BLOCKING RULES: This quick hitting reverse does not give the defenders in the box any blocking keys to assist them in reading reverse. **Base blocking rules.**

COACHING POINTS: This play is most effective versus a 7-man front that is playing a 3-deep rover coverage, or cover 2 corner-over toward the trips.

ASE: Blocks #1

AST: On, over, outside

ASG: On, over, reach, linebacker

C: Rule

BSG: Rule

BST: Rule

BSE: Downfield

QB: Reverse pivots and hastily fake the slant. He will not have time to make a great fake. Next, quickly deals the ball to the wingback and then fakes the keep.

ACE: Fakes the slant.

SB: Pulls and leads the wingback around end.

WB: Immediately gets to the mesh point and then races around end. Speed is one of the key elements of this play's success.

SE Rev

PLAY #30

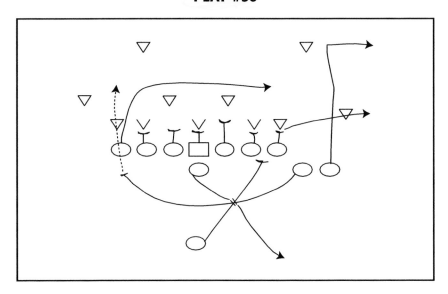

DESCRIPTION & BLOCKING RULES: This play-action pass features great misdirection and is effective versus any type of secondary coverage. **Standard pass pro blocking rules.**

COACHING POINTS: One of the advantages of the slant series from a trips formation is that it enables the offense to fake or run an off-tackle play, fake or run a reverse, and also simultaneously releases pass receivers into the secondary. This play is an excellent example of this potential.

ASE: Blocks #1 for 3 counts and then runs a five-yard arrow into the flats.

AST: On, backside gap, hunt

ASG: On, backside gap, hunt

C: On, backside gap, hunt

BSG: On, backside gap, hunt

BST: On, backside gap, hunt

BSE: Runs a five-yard drag across the formation. Finds a window.

QB: Fakes the slant/reverse and continues to roll deep into the flats. Reads the defender responsible for flat coverage.

ACE: Fakes the off-tackle power and then blocks #1.

SB: Fakes the reverse.

WB: Runs an 18-yard out. Versus man or cover 2, sells the post before breaking his pattern outside.

PLAY #31

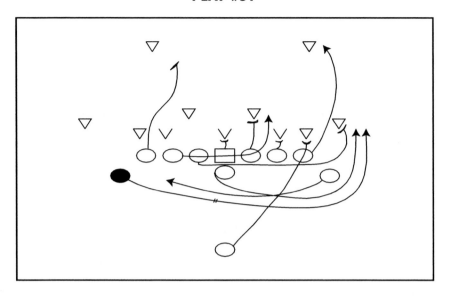

DESCRIPTION & BLOCKING RULES: This play is a double reverse. **Punch blocking rules.**

COACHING POINTS: This play is good to go to when the reverse has been used effectively. Because it has a high fumble potential, it should be practiced a few times each day.

ASE: Downfield

AST: On, over, outside

ASG: On, over, reach, tandem, linebacker

C: Gap, on, away

BSG: Gap, pulls and leads through the C gap

BST: Fill

BSE: Downfield

QB: Reverse pivots and make a quick fake to the aceback, hands the ball to the wingback, and momentarily fakes the quarterback keep before serving as a lead blocker.

ACE: Fakes the slant and then blocks #1.

SB: He is the ballcarrier. Secures the ball quickly and runs to daylight.

WB: After receiving the ball from the quarterback, immediately positions it in his left hand. Gently hands the ball to the slotback. Slamming the ball into the slotback's pouch is one of the leading causes of fumbles.

PLAY #32

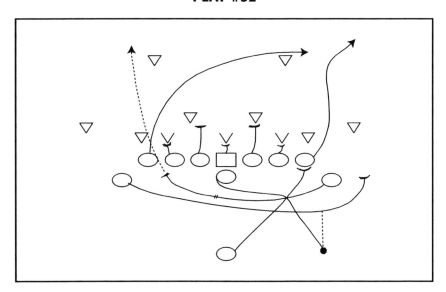

DESCRIPTION & BLOCKING RULES: This play is a double reverse pass. **Base blocking rules.**

COACHING POINTS: Although this pass involves only two receivers, the backfield misdirection frequently causes the defensive backs to lose track of these receivers.

ASE: Releases downfield and shows intent to block the safety versus cover 2 (versus cover 3, shows an intent to block the cornerback), but at the last minute, runs a flag pattern.

AST: On, over, outside

ASG: On, over, reach, tandem, linebacker

C: Rule

BSG: Rule

BST: Rule

BSE: Immediately releases toward the defender, whom the ASE is showing intent to block, and finds a window.

QB: Reverse pivots and makes a quick fake to the aceback, hands the ball to the wingback, and drops deep.

ACE: Fakes the slant and then blocks #1.

SB: After receiving the ball from the wingback, pitches it back to the quarterback, and then blocks frontside.

WB: After receiving the ball for the quarterback, immediately positions it in his left hand and gently gives it to the slotback. After the handoff, blocks backside. If everyone is blocked backside, streaks up the field.

PLAY #33

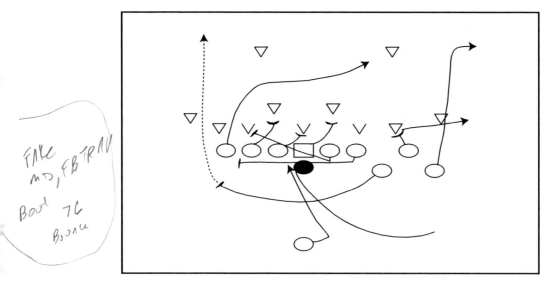

DESCRIPTION & BLOCKING RULES: This finesse play-action pass double-crosses defensive reads. **Otis blocking rules** (opposite the direction of the play).

COACHING POINTS: The aceback counter trey (Play 14), slotback reverse (Play 16), and naked boot (Play 15) can be incorporated into the slant series just as easily as they were incorporated into the power series. This play is a complement to the three previously mentioned plays. It has a concept similar to the naked boot because it leaves the 5 technique unblocked. The play is most effective versus a 7-man front that is playing a 3-deep rover coverage, or a balanced cover 2.

ASE: Blocks #1 for three counts and then releases shallow into the flats.

AST: Pulls opposite the play and blocks backside.

ASG: Pulls and traps opposite the play.

C: Away (exception: split-4)

BSG: Inside, linebacker (exception: split-4)

BST: If the guard is covered, blocks on, over, outside. If the guard is uncovered, blocks linebacker.

BSE: Run a 15-yard drag across the formation.

QB: Fakes the aceback counter trey, rolls deep, and reads the defender responsible for primary run support.

ACE: Fakes counter trey; aceback should make a great fake.

SB: Fakes the reverse and then blocks backside. If everyone is blocked backside, streaks up the field.

WB: Runs at the first defender outside of the ASE's block. Shows intent to block this defender and then runs an 18-yard out. (**Exception:** If this defender is blitzing, he will become the hot receiver and immediately run a five-yard out).

PLAY #34

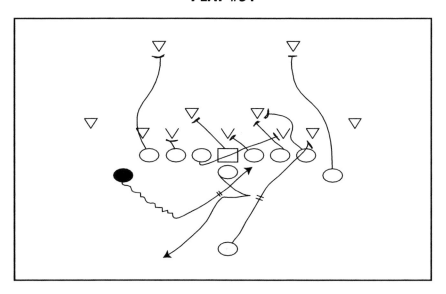

DESCRIPTION & BLOCKING RULES: This very quick hitting trap is set up by the slant. **Him trap blocking rules.**

COACHING POINTS: Quick motion into the backfield can be used to enhance the slant series. The last four plays in this chapter are illustrations of this tactic. This play double binds the 5 technique. If he closes inside to stop the trap, he is vulnerable to the slant and vice versa.

ASE: Him

AST: Him

ASG: Him

C: Him

BSG: Him

BST: Him

BSE: Downfield

QB: Reverse pivots and flashes the ball toward the aceback. He will not have time to fake to the aceback. Quickly turns back and gives the ball to the slotback, and then bootlegs away from the play.

ACE: Fakes the slant and blocks #1.

SB: Goes into quick motion and drives directly toward the mesh point. Hits the hole as quickly as possible and then levels off.

WB: Downfield

PLAY #35

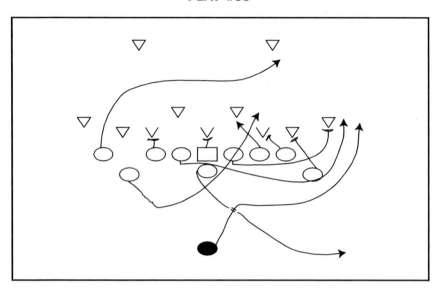

DESCRIPTION & BLOCKING RULES: This aceback bounce double-binds the 5 technique by giving him the same defensive read as the trap. **A variation of bounce blocking rules.**

COACHING POINTS: The wingback's crack block also double-binds the outside linebacker. It forces him to ask himself, "Should I close inside to stop the slant, or fight outside to stop the bounce?"

ASE: Inside, outside

AST: Inside, linebacker

ASG: Pull and lead

C: Gap, on, away

BSG: Gap, pull and lead

BST: Rule

BSE: Downfield

QB: Reverse pivots and deals the ball to the aceback as deep as possible, then fakes the quarterback keep.

ACE: His first step is a cross over step with his left foot. Next, steps with his right foot and then his left. He will have possession of the ball by the time he makes his third step. Plants on his third step and breaks the play outside. Runs to daylight.

SB: Goes into motion quickly and fakes the trap. The quarterback will not fake to him, but he can animate his fake by making a good pouch and slapping his right elbow with his left hand as he passes through the imaginary mesh point.

WB: Blocks #1 and caves him inside.

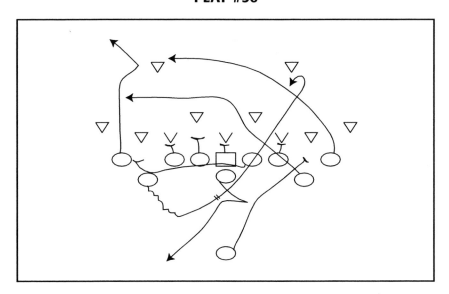

DESCRIPTION & BLOCKING RULES: This play-action pass features misdirection that is intended to momentarily freeze the inside linebackers and prevent them from adequately covering their hook zones. **Bootleg pass blocking rules.**

COACHING POINTS: This pass high-lows the hook zone away from the play fake (attackside is left).

ASE: Runs a post pattern versus cover 3, and a post-corner versus all other coverages.

AST: On, backside gap, hunt

ASG: On, backside gap, hunt

C: On, away

BSG: Pulls playside and blocks tandem, #1.

BST: Rule

BSE: Runs an 18-yard drag.

QB: Reverse pivots and flashes the ball toward the aceback. He will not have time to fake to the aceback. Quickly turns back and fakes the ball to the slotback, then sets deep to the left. Reads the inside linebackers and safety(s).

ACE: Fakes the slant and blocks #1.

SB: Goes into quick motion and hits the mesh point as quickly as possible. Blocks the inside linebacker if he blitzes; if he drops into coverage, finds a window in the hook zone.

WB: Runs a five-yard drag across the formation.

PLAY #37

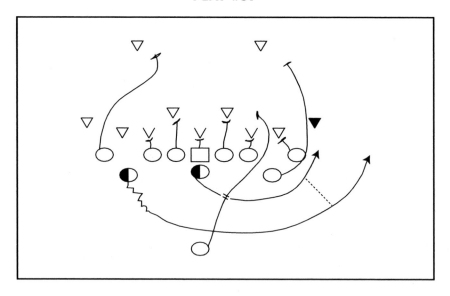

DESCRIPTION & BLOCKING RULES: This play fakes the slant and options the DB responsible for primary run support. **Base blocking rules.**

COACHING POINTS: This play is an easy play for even a non-option quarterback to execute.

ASE: Blocks #1

AST: On, over, outside

ASG: On, over, reach, tandem, linebacker

C: Rule

BSG: Rule

BST: Rule

BSE: Downfield

QB: Reverse pivots and fakes the slant. Attacks the perimeter and options the DB who is responsible for primary run support.

ACE: Fakes the slant and seals inside linebacker pursuit.

SB: Goes into quick motion at a depth that will enable him to establish and maintain a good pitch relationship with the quarterback.

WB: Downfield

7

The Sprint-Out Series

Today, coaches, players, and audiences are witnessing a very exciting trend in football: the utilization of fleet footed mobile quarterbacks who can threaten the perimeter and run the ball almost as well as they can throw it. Although long overdue, this trend adds a thrilling new dimension to the passing game, and severely burdens the defense. This series is intended to accommodate the needs of this exhilarating new breed of quarterbacks.

PLAY #38

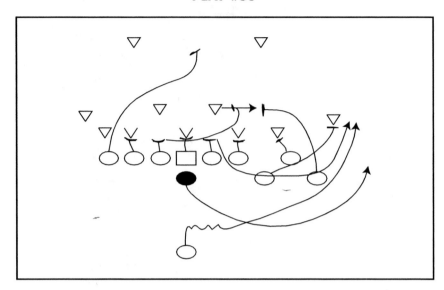

LA W
QB ball K
MO

QB
Sweep

DESCRIPTION & BLOCKING RULES: This is a predetermined quarterback run. **Base blocking rules.**

COACHING POINTS: The offensive line will set playside and pass block. When assigned to block a linebacker, a lineman will wash out the linebacker if he blitzes. However, if the linebacker drops into coverage, the lineman will pull and turn upfield to block.

ASE: Cracks on #1.

AST: On, over, outside

ASG: On, over, reach, tandem, linebacker

C: Rule

BSG: Rule

BST: Rule

BSE: Rule

QB: Opens up at a 45-degree angle and gains depth as he begins his course to the perimeter. It is imperative that he initially shows pass by carrying the ball in a passing position.

ACE: Goes into quick motion and leads the quarterback around the corner.

SB: Blocks the DB responsible for primary run support.

WB: Seals inside linebacker pursuit.

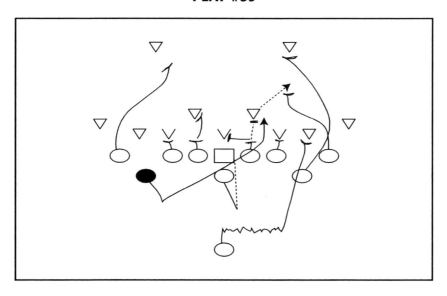

DESCRIPTION & BLOCKING RULES: This play is the shovel pass. **Him blocking rules.**

COACHING POINTS: All linemen will show pass at the snap. Versus the 3-4, the ASG will block the inside linebacker if he blitzes. If the linebacker drops into coverage, the ASG will double-team the nose tackle with the center.

ASE: Releases downfield and blocks the inside linebacker if he drops into coverage. If the linebacker blitzes, ASE blocks downfield.

AST: Him

ASG: Him

C: Him

BSG: Him

BST: Him

BSE: Downfield

QB: Opens up at a 45-degree angle, shows pass, and takes three steps. On his third step (right foot), he stops abruptly and tosses a gentle pass to the slotback. If he senses a bad play, quarterback throws the ball into the dirt and wastes the down.

ACE: Goes into quick motion and blocks #1.

SB: Drives for the outside foot of the ASG. Immediately secures the ball after the catch and reads the guard's block.

WB: Downfield

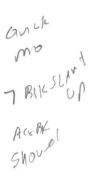

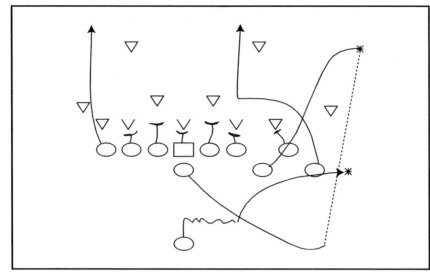

DESCRIPTION & BLOCKING RULES: This version of the shovel pass gives the quarterback four pass options. **Base blocking rules.**

COACHING POINTS: It is important that the offensive line does not go downfield.

ASE: Cracks on #1.

AST: On, over, outside

ASG: On, over, reach, tandem, linebacker

C: Rule

BSG: Rule

BST: Rule

BSE: Runs a skinny post

QB: Opens up at a 45-degree angle and gains depth as he begins his course to the perimeter. He will option the DB responsible for primary run support. He has the option of an aceback shovel, a seven-yard out to the slotback, or a deep pattern to the wingback or backside end.

ACE: Goes into quick motion and runs a shovel route parallel to the line of scrimmage.

SB: Runs a seven-yard out.

WB: Runs directly at the inside linebacker. Gets his attention and tries to get linebacker to momentarily jam him. Next, streaks down the field toward the safety prepared to block or receive the pass.

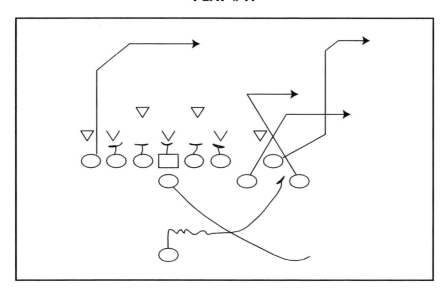

DESCRIPTION & BLOCKING RULES: This sprint-out pass features a number of rubs that put great pressure on man coverage. **Standard pass pro blocking rules.**

COACHING POINTS: This pattern can also be used to attack zone coverages because it high-lows the flats. This pattern is not good when a cover 2 team plays corner-over versus trips (unless they are playing man coverage).

ASE: Gets upfield after running a quick arrow and sells a flag pattern. At about 16 yards, turns the flag into an out.

AST: On, backside gap, hunt

ASG: On, backside gap, hunt

C: On, backside gap, hunt

BSG: On, backside gap, hunt

BST: On, backside gap, hunt

BSE: Runs a backside dig pattern.

QB: Reverse pivots at a 45-degree angle and gains depth as he attacks the perimeter and reads the coverage.

ACE: Goes into quick motion and blocks #1.

SB: Rubs behind the wingback and runs a five-yard out.

WB: Rubs on top of the slotback and runs an inside arrow. At a depth of seven yards, turns his pattern into an out.

PLAY #42

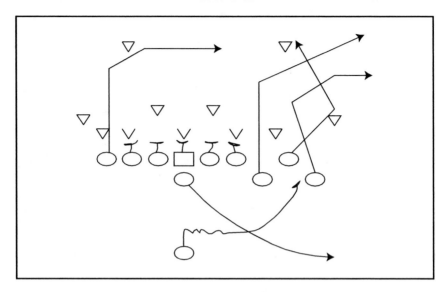

DESCRIPTION & BLOCKING RULES: This pattern is most effective versus cover 2. **Standard pass pro blocking rules.**

COACHING POINTS: Although no high-lows occur, the rubs can cause considerable problems for man coverage. This pattern is not good when a cover 2 team plays corner-over versus trips (unless they are playing man coverage).

ASE: Turns his five-yard arrow into a post. Versus cover 2, his assignment is to freeze the free safety so that the slotback's flag pattern will sneak behind the cornerback.

AST: On, backside gap, hunt

ASG: On, backside gap, hunt

C: On, backside gap, hunt

BSG: On, backside gap, hunt

BST: On, backside gap, hunt

BSE: Runs a backside dig pattern.

QB: Reverse pivots at a 45-degree angle, and gains depth as he attacks the perimeter and reads the coverage.

ACE: Goes into quick motion and blocks #1.

SB: Runs a flag pattern.

WB: Cuts his in-out arrow pattern into a 10-yard out.

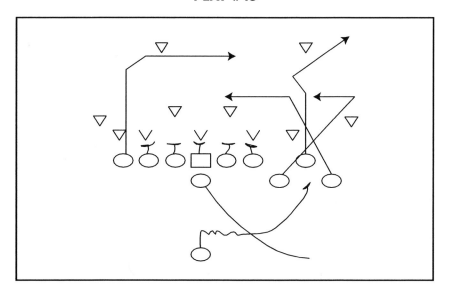

DESCRIPTION & BLOCKING RULES: This pattern attacks any zone coverage because it creates a high-low of the hook zones. **Standard pass pro blocking rules.**

COACHING POINTS: The slotback-wingback rub can also be deadly versus man coverage.

ASE: Runs a post-corner pattern versus man and cover 2, and a post pattern versus cover 3.

AST: On, backside gap, hunt

ASG: On, backside gap, hunt

C: On, backside gap, hunt

BSG: On, backside gap, hunt

BST: On, backside gap, hunt

BSE: Runs a backside dig pattern.

QB: Reverse pivots at a 45-degree angle and gains depth as he attacks the perimeter and reads the coverage.

ACE: Goes into quick motion and blocks #1.

SB: Rubs behind the wingback and runs a seven-yard arrow-and-in pattern.

WB: Rubs on top of the slotback and runs a five-yard arrow-in-and-drag pattern.

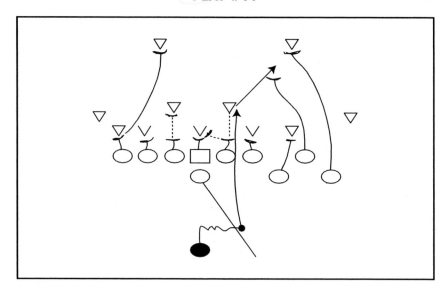

DESCRIPTION & BLOCKING RULES: This play is a sprint draw. **Him blocking rules.**

COACHING POINTS: All linemen will show pass at the snap. Versus the 3-4, the ASG will block the inside linebacker if he blitzes. If the linebacker drops into coverage, the ASG will double-team the nose tackle with the center.

ASE: Releases downfield and blocks the inside linebacker if he drops into coverage. If the linebacker blitzes, blocks downfield.

AST: Him

ASG: Him

C: Him

BSG: Him

BST: Him

BSE: Downfield

QB: Opens up at a 45-degree angle, shows pass, and deals the ball to the aceback.

ACE: Goes into quick motion and shows intent to block. As the quarterback nears him, squares his shoulders to the line, receives the ball and reads the guard's block as he runs to daylight.

SB: Blocks #1.

WB: Downfield

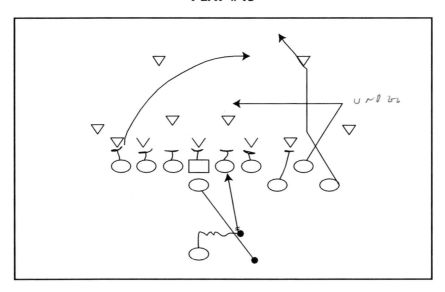

DESCRIPTION & BLOCKING RULES: This play is a fake draw pass. **Standard pass pro blocking rules.**

COACHING POINTS: The fake draw should freeze the inside linebackers and enable the receivers to high-low the hook zones.

ASE: Rubs on top of the wingback and runs an arrow-out-drag pattern at a depth of five yards.

AST: On, backside gap, hunt

ASG: On, backside gap, hunt

C: On, backside gap, hunt

BSG: On, backside gap, hunt

BST: On, backside gap, hunt

BSE: Slams #1 and then runs a 15-yard banana route.

QB: Opens up at a 45-degree angle, shows pass, and fakes the ball to the aceback. Sets three more steps and reads the linebackers.

ACE: Goes into quick motion and fakes the sprint draw. Makes a great fake.

SB: Blocks #1.

WB: Rubs behind the end and runs an arrow-in-post pattern.

8

The Belly Series

The belly series is another aceback adaptation of one of football's oldest series. Each play in this series will begin by having the wingback go into quick motion and immediately strike at the heart of the defense. The sequential complements enhance the base play by adding misdirection that pressures all sectors of the defense.

PLAY #46

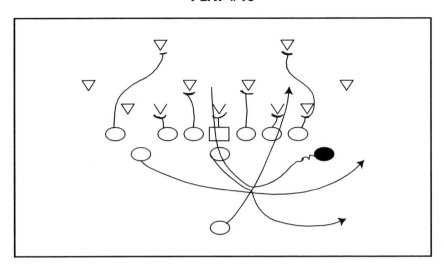

DESCRIPTION & BLOCKING RULES: This play is the base play of the series. Its strength is that the blocking scheme gives the defense no clue as to who is getting the ball, the wingback or the aceback. **Base blocking rules.**

COACHING POINTS: The motion has to be timed in such a way that the quarterback will reverse pivot and immediately give the ball to the wingback. The aceback's path will trail the wingback's path and enable the quarterback to then fake to the aceback. After this fake, the slotback will trail the aceback and threaten the perimeter.

ASE: Slams #1 and then blocks downfield.

AST: On, over, outside

ASG: On, over, reach, tandem, linebacker

C: Rule

BSG: Rule

BST: Rule

BSE: Downfield

QB: First, steps straight back with his right foot. Next, reverse pivots on his right foot and hands the ball to the wingback. Fakes the slant to the aceback and then fakes the keep with the slotback leading.

ACE: Fakes the slant.

SB: Trails slightly behind the quarterback's fake to the aceback and pretends to lead the quarterback to the perimeter.

WB: Goes into quick motion. Receives the handoff from the quarterback and immediately secures the ball with both hands. Versus an odd defense, reads the center's block. Versus an even defense, reads the BSG's block.

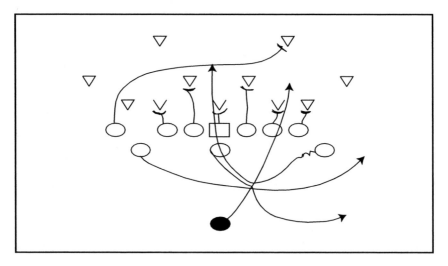

DESCRIPTION & BLOCKING RULES: This play is the next sequence in the series. **Base blocking rules.**

COACHING POINTS: The base blocking rules give the defense no clue as to who is getting the ball. Some coaches, however, may desire to occasionally run the play with either a slant or zone scheme.

ASE: Blocks #1

AST: On, over, outside

ASG: On, over, reach, tandem, linebacker

C: Rule

BSG: Rule

BST: Rule

BSE: Downfield

QB: Simultaneously seats the ball (to hide it from the defense) as he steps straight back with his right foot. Next, reverse pivots on his right foot and continues to seat the ball. He will not have time to make a fake to the wingback; the fake is the wingback's responsibility. Now, hands the ball to the aceback and then fakes the keep with the slotback leading.

ACE: Runs directly at the hole. Secures the ball after the handoff and runs to daylight.

SB: Trails slightly behind the quarterback's fake to the aceback and pretends to lead the quarterback to the perimeter.

WB: Goes into quick motion. As he passes through the mesh point for Play #46, makes a great fake by slapping his left elbow with his right hand. Sells his fake by continuing his course with the same intensity that he would if he had been given the ball.

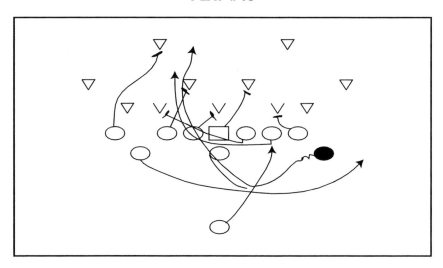

DESCRIPTION & BLOCKING RULES: This play is the same as Play #46, with the exception of the blocking scheme. **Otis blocking rules**

COACHING POINTS: Frequently, the BST is not quick enough to lead. If this is the case, trap blocking rules can be substituted for the recommended scheme.

ASE: Downfield

AST: If the guard is covered, blocks on, over, outside. If the guard is uncovered, blocks linebacker.

ASG: Inside, linebacker (exception: split-4)

C: Away (exception: split-4)

BSG: Pull and trap

BST: Pull and lead

BSE: Fills inside.

QB: First, steps directly back with his right foot. Next, reverse pivots on his right foot and hands the ball to the wingback. Fakes the slant to the aceback and then fakes the keep with the slotback leading.

ACE: Fakes the slant.

SB: Trails slightly behind the quarterback's fake to the aceback and pretends to lead the quarterback to the perimeter.

WB: Goes into quick motion. Receives the handoff from the quarterback and immediately secures the ball with both hands. Continues securing the ball with two hands as he reads the blocks of the BSG and BST.

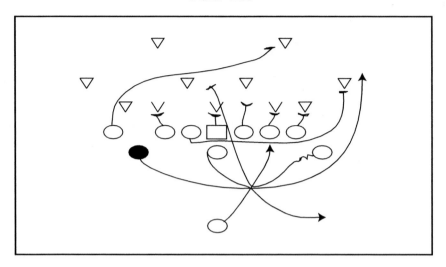

DESCRIPTION & BLOCKING RULES: This play is the slotback belly. **Punch blocking rules.**

COACHING POINTS: A quarterback keep (not illustrated) can also be added to this series. Although bounce blocking rules can also be used for this play, punch rules give the flowside defenders no clue as to who has the ball.

ASE: Blocks #1

AST: On, over, outside

ASG: On, over, reach, tandem, linebacker

C: Gap, on, away

BSG: Gap, pull and lead through the C gap

BST: Fill

BSE: Downfield

QB: Seats the ball as he steps directly back with his right foot. Next, reverse pivots on his right foot as he continues seating the ball. He will not have time to make a fake to the wingback, but he will have time to fake to the aceback. Next, hands the ball to the slotback and then drops deep and fakes a play-action pass.

ACE: Fakes the slant.

SB: Trails slightly behind the quarterback's fake to the aceback and immediately secures the ball as he attacks the perimeter.

WB: Goes into quick motion. As he passes through the mesh point for Play #46, makes a great fake by slapping his left elbow with his right hand. Sells his fake by continuing his course with the same intensity that he would if he had been given the ball.

PLAY #50

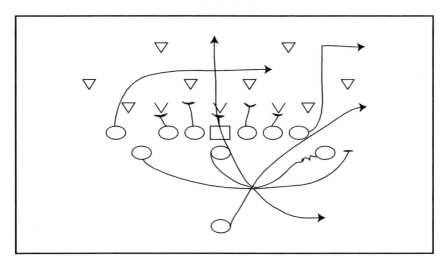

DESCRIPTION & BLOCKING RULES: This play is one of the series' play-action passes. Although only three play-action passes have been illustrated, obviously many more could be included. **Standard pass pro blocking rules.**

COACHING POINTS: The purpose of this pass is to high–low the flats. This pattern is not good if a cover 2 secondary employs a corners-over look.

ASE: Runs an 18-yard out.

AST: On, backside gap, hunt

ASG: On, backside gap, hunt

C: On, backside gap, hunt

BSG: On, backside gap, hunt

BST: On, backside gap, hunt

BSE: Runs a five-yard drag across the formation.

QB: Maneuvers exactly as he did when he faked the slotback belly. After this fake, rolls playside and reads the defender responsible for flat coverage.

ACE: Fakes the slant and runs a five-yard out.

SB: Trails slightly behind the quarterback's fake to the aceback and blocks #1.

WB: Goes into quick motion and fakes Play #46. After his fake, streaks down the center of the field (favors the playside free safety).

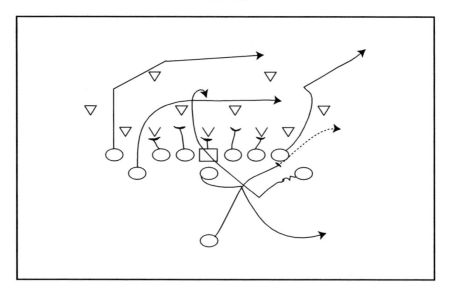

DESCRIPTION & BLOCKING RULES: This play is the series' second play-action pass. **Standard pass pro blocking rules.**

COACHING POINT: The purpose of this pass is to high–low the hook zones.

ASE: Runs a flag route versus covers 1 and 2, and a post versus cover 3.

AST: On, backside gap, hunt

ASG: On, backside gap, hunt

C: On, backside gap, hunt

BSG: On, backside gap, hunt

BST: On, backside gap, hunt

BSE: Runs a dig pattern.

QB: Maneuvers exactly as he did when he faked the slotback belly. After his fake, rolls playside and reads the inside linebackers.

ACE: Fakes the slant and blocks #1.

SB: Runs a five-yard drag across the formation.

WB: Goes into quick motion and fakes Play #46. After his fake, finds a five-yard window between the tackles.

PLAY #52

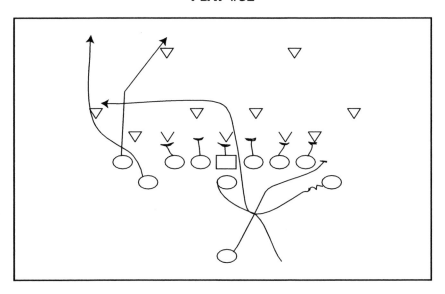

DESCRIPTION & BLOCKING RULES: This play is the series' last play-action pass. The protection is right even though the pass patterns are opposite the protection. **Standard pass pro blocking rules** (attackside is left).

COACHING POINT: This throwback pass is particularly effective versus cover 2. Because it has four attackside blockers, it is particularly effective versus a corners-over cover 2 that attempts to blitz one of the cornerbacks.

ASE: Blocks #1

AST: On, backside gap, hunt

ASG: On, backside gap, hunt

C: On, backside gap, hunt

BSG: On, backside gap, hunt

BST: On, backside gap, hunt

BSE: Runs a post pattern.

QB: Maneuvers exactly as he did when he faked the slotback belly. After this fake, rolls right and reads the free safety.

ACE: Fakes the slant and blocks outside of the ASE's block.

SB: Runs out-and-up pattern.

WB: Goes into quick motion and fakes Play #46. After his fake, runs a five-yard out.

9

The Sweep Series

This series is a conglomeration that incorporates I formation and wing-T principles. Each back (aceback, wingback, and slotback) is used as one of the primary ballcarriers in this series. Power, misdirection, and double-binding are the hallmarks of the sweep series.

PLAY #53

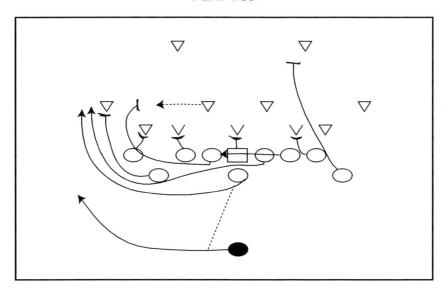

DESCRIPTION & BLOCKING RULES: This play is a variation of John McKay's student body left. **Punch blocking rules.**

COACHING POINTS: The defense must put a defender between the tight end and slotback, or relinquish two gaps. This defender is usually prey for the tight end's crack block. The ASG will pull and cut off the pursuit of any linebacker that he is assigned to block.

ASE: Blocks #1

AST: On, over, outside

ASG: On, over, reach, tandem, linebacker

C: Gap, on, away

BSG: Gap, pull and lead through the C gap

BST: Fill

BSE: Downfield

QB: First, jab steps (parallel to the line of scrimmage) with his left foot. Next reverse pivots on his left foot and simultaneously tosses the ball to the aceback. Now, leads the pack into the end zone.

ACE: Steps parallel to the line of scrimmage with his left foot. Locks the ball into his hands as he receives the toss from the quarterback. Immediately secures the ball with his left hand and finds the end zone.

SB: Pulls and blocks the defensive back responsible for primary run support.

WB: Downfield

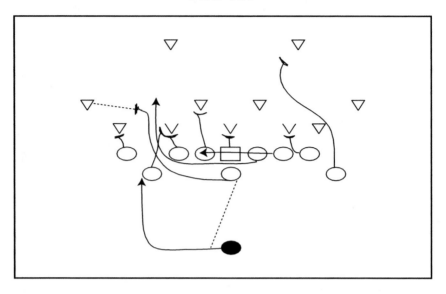

DESCRIPTION & BLOCKING RULES: This play is the off-tackle version of student body left. **Weakside power blocking rules.**

COACHING POINTS: Occasionally, a team will concede both the C and D gaps in an attempt to reinforce containment and avoid the tight end's crack block. When this occurs, this play is the next logical succession.

ASE: Blocks #1

AST: Rule

ASG: Rule

C: On, Away

BSG: Pulls and leads, looks inside, and then downfield.

BST: Fill

BSE: Downfield

QB: Steps as he did on the sweep and tosses the ball to the aceback. As he leads through the hole, he should be shoulder-to-shoulder with the pulling guard. He will look first to the outside and then downfield in determining whom he should block.

ACE: Steps parallel to the line of scrimmage with his left foot and sells sweep. When he gets perpendicular to the hole, makes an abrupt 90-degree cut toward the point of attack. Attacks the hole with his shoulders parallel to the line so that he will be able to cut in any direction.

SB: Blocks #2

WB: Downfield

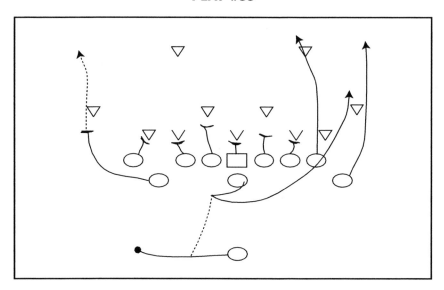

DESCRIPTION & BLOCKING RULES: This aceback pass is effective when the defense is geared up to stop the sweep. **Standard pass pro blocking rules** (attackside is left)**.**

COACHING POINT: Many times the defense will forget to cover the quarterback when employing man coverage. This pattern will exploit this oversight.

ASE: Blocks #1

AST: On, backside gap, hunt

ASG: On, backside gap, hunt

C: On, backside gap, hunt

BSG: On, backside gap, hunt

BST: On, backside gap, hunt

BSE: Runs a skinny post.

QB: After he tosses the ball to the aceback, reverses direction and runs a funnel pattern between the tight end and wingback.

ACE: Sells sweep for a few steps after receiving the toss. Then stops and looks backside.

SB: Releases outside and blocks the DB assigned primary run support if he is attacking the line of scrimmage to stop the sweep. If he is playing soft, runs a flag pattern.

WB: Streaks up the field, making certain to gain considerable vertical stretch between himself and the end.

PLAY #56

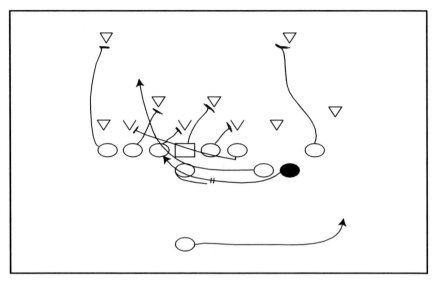

DESCRIPTION & BLOCKING RULES: This quick hitting counter employs **Tackle trap blocking rules.**

COACHING POINTS: Rather than using counter trey blocking rules, this play uses a scheme that has the tackle trapping and the slotback leading the ballcarrier through the hole. This blocking scheme is especially effective versus the split defense.

ASE: Downfield

AST: Over, tandem, linebacker

ASG: Gap, stack, inside, linebacker

C: On, over, away

BSG: On, over, backside gap, tandem

BST: Pull and trap

BSE: Downfield

QB: First, takes a jab step straight back with his right foot; this will enable him to gain enough depth to allow the wingback a clear path to the hole. Makes sure to seat the ball securely as he takes this jab step. Next, pivots on his right foot so that his left foot is pointing at about five o'clock. As he pivots, fakes a pitch to the aceback and then deals the ball to the wingback.

ACE: Fakes the sweep.

SB: Pulls and leads through the hole.

WB: After receiving the handoff, immediately secures the ball and keeps it protected with both hands until he is out of traffic.

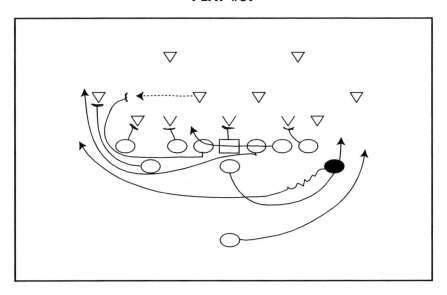

DESCRIPTION & BLOCKING RULES: This play is a wingback sweep. **Punch blocking rules.**

COACHING POINTS: The action of the quarterback and wingback sets up Play #58, an explosive misdirection play.

ASE: Crack blocks #1

AST: On, over, outside

ASG: On, over, reach, tandem, linebacker

C: Gap, on, away

BSG: Gap, pulls and leads through the C gap

BST: Fill

BSE: Inside

QB: Opens up toward the wingback, hands him the ball, and then bootlegs away from the play. Does not gain depth as he bootlegs; makes his course flat.

ACE: Runs opposite the play, establishing a pitch relationship with the quarterback.

SB: Pull and lead

WB: Goes into quick motion, receives the handoff from the quarterback, secures the ball with his left hand and reads the block of the slotback and BSG.

PLAY #58

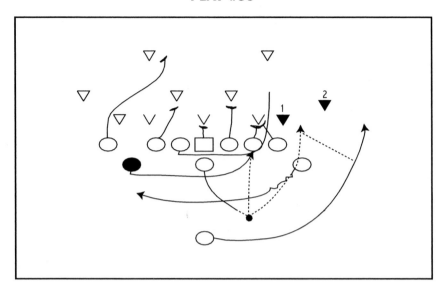

DESCRIPTION & BLOCKING RULES: This play is a shovel/option that attacks both the off-tackle hole and the perimeter. **Power blocking rules.**

COACHING POINTS: If the quarterback sees that outside linebacker is aggressively playing the shovel, he can continue into the perimeter with the option to pitch the ball to the aceback.

ASE: Blocks #2

AST: Rule

ASG: Rule

C: On, Away

BSG: Pull and lead

BST: Blocks inside

BSE: Downfield

QB: Opens up toward the wingback and fakes the handoff. Momentarily hides the ball on his right hip as he fades back and reads the play of the outside linebacker. If the linebacker aggressively closes the off-tackle hole, quarterback continues to bootleg and options the cornerback. If the outside linebacker attacks him, he shovel passes to the slotback.

ACE: Establishes a pitch relationship with the quarterback.

SB: Runs a shovel route through the C gap.

WB: Goes into quick motion and fakes the sweep.

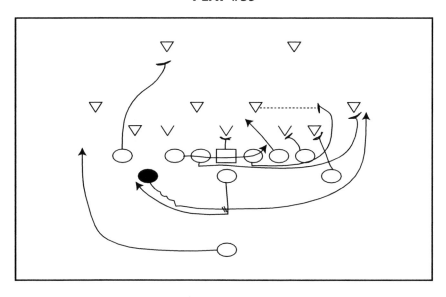

DESCRIPTION & BLOCKING RULES: This play is the slotback sweep. **Bounce blocking rules.**

COACHING POINTS: This play sets up a number of other plays that could prove to be game breakers.

ASE: Inside, linebacker

AST: Inside, linebacker

ASG: Pull and lead (looks for the inside linebacker)

C: Gap, on, away

BSG: Gap, pull and lead

BST: Fill

BSE: Downfield

QB: Opens up toward the slotback, hands him the ball, and then bootlegs away from the play.

ACE: Runs opposite the play, establishing a pitch relationship with the quarterback.

SB: Goes into quick motion, receives the handoff from the quarterback, secures the ball with his right hand, and reads the block of the BSG.

WB: Blocks #1

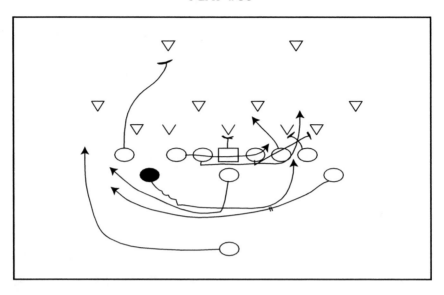

DESCRIPTION & BLOCKING RULES: This off-tackle version of the slotback sweep features misdirection. **Slant blocking rules.**

COACHING POINTS: It is vital that the slotback sell sweep and not make his cut toward the hole until he is perpendicular to it. This play can also be run without the misdirection. The wingback can influence #1 and double-bind his sweep/off-tackle read, or the wingback can release downfield for the purpose of confusing the secondaries' pass/run read.

ASE: Blocks #2

AST: Inside, linebacker

ASG: Pulls and traps #1

C: Gap, on, away

BSG: Gap, pull and lead

BST: Fills if the guard pulls (listens for his call); otherwise, blocks rule.

BSE: Downfield

QB: Opens up toward the slotback, hands him the ball, and then bootlegs away from the play.

ACE: Runs opposite the play, establishing a pitch relationship with the quarterback.

SB: Goes into quick motion, receives the handoff from the quarterback, secures the ball with his right hand, and reads the block of the BSG. He need not fake the ball to the wingback.

WB: Fakes the reverse.

PLAY #61

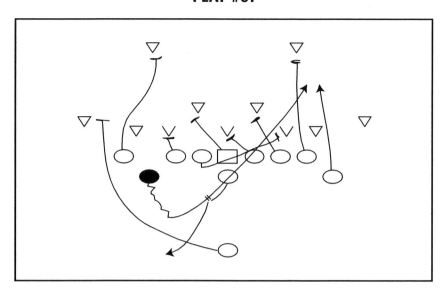

DESCRIPTION & BLOCKING RULES: This play is a slotback trap. **Him blocking.**

COACHING POINTS: The down block of the AST and the influence block of the ASE put the playside 5 technique in a double-bind situation.

ASE: Him

AST: Him

ASG: Him

C: Him

BSG: Him

BST: Him

BSE: Him

QB: Opens up toward the slotback, hands him the ball, and then bootlegs away from the play.

ACE: Runs opposite the play.

SB: Goes into quick motion, receives the handoff from the quarterback, and secures the ball with both hands as he immediately bursts through traffic.

WB: Downfield

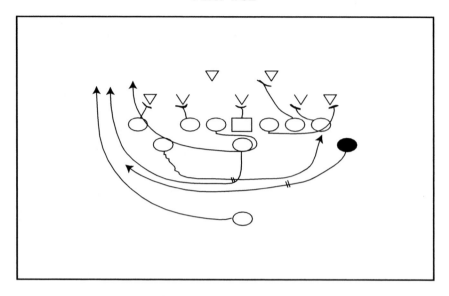

DESCRIPTION & BLOCKING RULES: This play is a reverse that complements the slotback sweep. **Variation of slant blocking rules** (opposite the play's direction).

COACHING POINTS: Because of its blocking scheme, this play is what the old timers would refer to as a sucker play.

ASE: Inside

AST: Rule

ASG: Pretends to pull, reverses direction, and leads.

C: Gap, on, away

BSG: Gap, pulls and blocks #1 backside.

BST: Inside, linebacker

BSE: Fill

QB: Opens up toward the slotback, hands him the ball, and then leads the wingback into the perimeter.

ACE: The quarterback and the aceback are the lead blockers.

SB: Goes into quick motion, receives the handoff from the quarterback, and immediately hands it off to the wingback.

WB: He is the ballcarrier. Receives the handoff from the slotback and reads the blocks of the quarterback and aceback.

PLAY #63

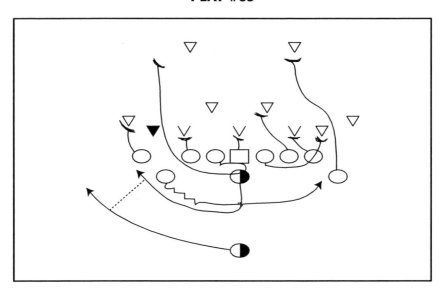

DESCRIPTION & BLOCKING RULES: This play is an option away from the slotback sweep. **Variation of slant blocking rules** (opposite the play's direction).

COACHING POINTS: This play also relies upon the same sucker play principles as Play #62. Coaches who may not feel secure about this blocking scheme may wish to run the play using punch blocking rules. It should also be noted that sucker plays work well versus a disciplined reading defense, but are seldom worth a penny versus an unpredictable blitzing defense.

ASE: Blocks the DB responsible for primary run support.

AST: Rule

ASG: Pretends to pull, reverses direction, and leads.

C: Gap, on, away

BSG: Gap, pulls and blocks #1 backside.

BST: Inside, linebacker

BSE: Fill

QB: Opens up toward the slotback, fakes the handoff, bootlegs playside, and then options #1.

ACE: Establishes a pitch relationship with the quarterback.

SB: Goes into quick motion and fakes the sweep.

WB: Downfield

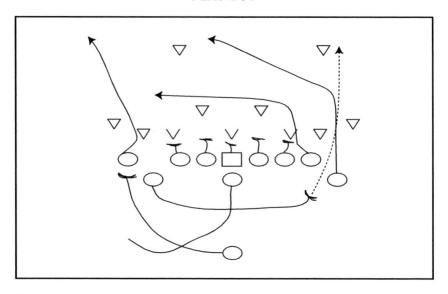

DESCRIPTION & BLOCKING RULES: This play is a bootleg pass that is established by the slotback sweep. **Standard pass pro blocking rules.**

COACHING POINTS: The wingback will adjust his pattern according to the coverage.

ASE: Slams #1 and runs toward the flag.

AST: On, backside gap, hunt

ASG: On, backside gap, hunt

C: On, backside gap, hunt

BSG: On, backside gap, hunt

BST: On, backside gap, hunt

BSE: Runs a five-yard drag.

QB: Opens up toward the slotback, fakes the handoff, and then gains depth as he bootlegs. Reads the inside linebackers and safety(s). The wingback is his primary target, and the BSE is his secondary choice.

ACE: Blocks #1

SB: Goes into quick motion, fakes the sweep and blocks #1 backside. If #1 drops into coverage, streaks up the field.

WB: Runs a post versus cover 2, and a dig versus everything else.

10

The Quick Pitch Series

The quick pitch is a play whose roots find themselves in the era of leather helmets and handlebar mustaches. Although antiquated, this play will always have a prominent place in the modern game because it enables an offense to strike the perimeter with lightning quickness.

PLAY #65

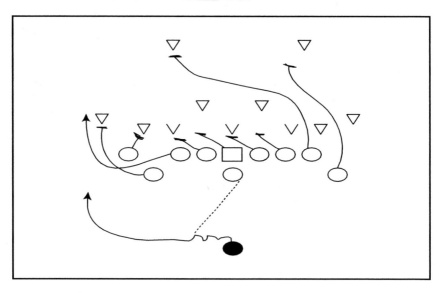

DESCRIPTION & BLOCKING RULES: This play is the quick pitch, the base play of the series. **Him blocking rules.**

COACHING POINTS: This play requires three to four reps daily.

ASE: Crack blocks #1

AST: Pull and lead. His first step should be at seven o'clock.

ASG: Scoops playside.

C: Scoops playside.

BSG: Scoops playside.

BST: Scoops playside.

BSE: Downfield

QB: Reverse pivots and pitches the ball to the aceback. His pitch should be a dead ball—not a spiral or an end-over-end pitch. After he pitches it, the quarterback follows the ball and prepares to recover it.

ACE: Goes into quick motion. At the snap, bellies back slightly. Locks the ball into his hands as he receives the pitch, and immediately secures it in his left hand. Aceback should be prepared to recover a bad pitch; remember, the ball is live.

SB: Pulls and blocks the cornerback.

WB: Downfield

PLAY #66

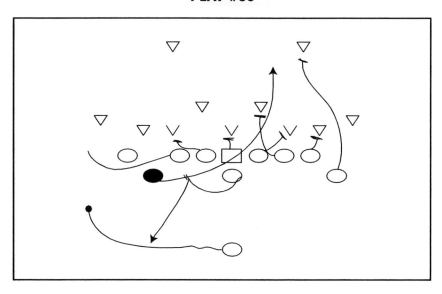

DESCRIPTION & BLOCKING RULES: This sucker play exploits the quick defensive pursuit that is needed to stop the quick pitch. **Him blocking rules.**

COACHING POINTS: The fake of the quarterback and the aceback are the most important elements of this play.

ASE: Downfield

AST: Him

ASG: Him

C: Him

BSG: Him

BST: Pulls and pretends to lead.

BSE: Slams #1 and blocks downfield.

QB: Reverse pivots and pretends to pitch the ball to the aceback. Brings the ball back to his body and immediately hands the ball to the slotback.

ACE: Goes into quick motion and fakes catching the ball as the quarterback pretends to pitch it to him.

SB: Aims for the playside A gap. Secures the ball with both hands as he explodes through traffic.

WB: Downfield

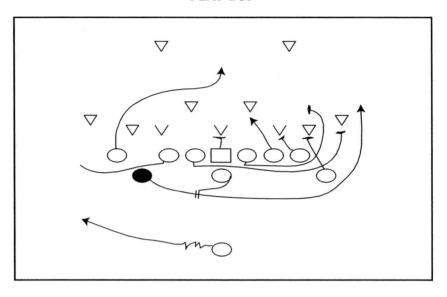

DESCRIPTION & BLOCKING RULES: This play is a reverse that fakes quick pitch. **Variation of bounce blocking rules.**

COACHING POINTS: This play is slightly easier to execute than Play #66. It also enables the quarterback an instant longer to exaggerate his fake.

ASE: Inside, linebacker

AST: Inside, linebacker

ASG: Pull and lead, look for the inside linebacker.

C: Gap, on, away

BSG: Gap, pull and lead

BST: Pulls and pretends to lead the quick pitch.

BSE: Downfield

QB: Reverse pivots and pretends to pitch the ball to the aceback. Allows the ball to remain extended as the slotback runs through it.

ACE: Goes into quick motion and fakes catching the ball as the quarterback pretends to pitch it to him.

SB: Bellies back slightly and runs through the ball. Secures the ball in his right hand as he attacks the perimeter.

WB: Blocks #1

PLAY #68

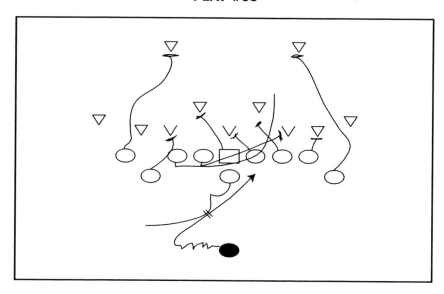

DESCRIPTION & BLOCKING RULES: This aceback counter employs fake quick pitch action. **Otis blocking rules**.

COACHING POINTS: The BSE's block simulates the crack action of his quick pitch assignment.

ASE: Blocks #1

AST: If the guard is covered, blocks on, over, outside. If the guard is uncovered, blocks linebacker.

ASG: Inside, linebacker (exception: split-4)

C: Away (exception: split-4)

BSG: Pull and trap

BST: Pull and lead

BSE: Slams #1 and blocks downfield.

QB: After reverse pivoting and pretending to pitch to the aceback, gains depth and quickly deals the ball to the aceback.

ACE: Goes into quick motion but stops abruptly as the ball is hiked and directs his course toward the ASG. Receives the ball from the quarterback and secures it with both hands as he blasts through traffic.

SB: Fills inside.

WB: Downfield

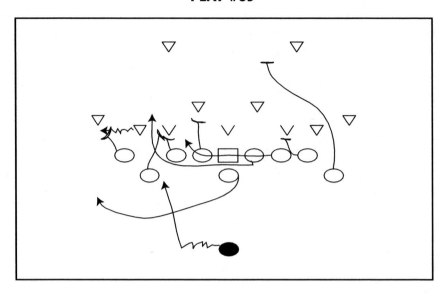

DESCRIPTION & BLOCKING RULES: This off-tackle play fakes quick pitch action. **Power blocking rules**

COACHING POINTS: When the quick pitch is gaining good yardage, the outside linebacker will frequently move outside of the tight end when he sees aceback motion. This play exploits this defensive tactic.

ASE: Blocks #1

AST: Rule

ASG: Rule

C: On, Away

BSG: Pull and lead

BST: Fill

BSE: Downfield

QB: After reverse pivoting and pretending to pitch to the aceback, gains width and depth and quickly deals the ball to the aceback. Then fakes a quarterback keep.

ACE: Goes into quick motion, stops abruptly as the ball is hiked and directs his course toward the off-tackle hole. Receives the ball from the quarterback and secures it with both hands until he is out of traffic.

SB: Blocks #2

WB: Downfield

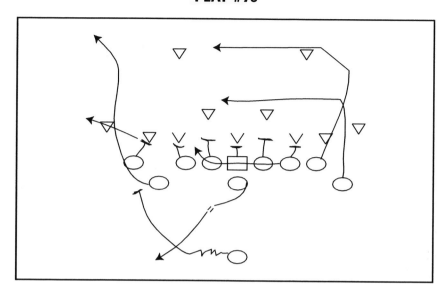

DESCRIPTION & BLOCKING RULES: This play is one of the series' play-action passes. **Standard pass pro blocking rules.**

COACHING POINTS: This pass will high–low the backside hook zones. Also, the release of the ASE and slotback will create a natural rub, which will be effective versus man coverage.

ASE: Slams #1 and runs a five-yard out into the flats. His course will create a rub behind the slotback's release.

AST: On, backside gap, hunt

ASG: On, backside gap, hunt

C: On, backside gap, hunt

BSG: On, backside gap, hunt

BST: On, backside gap, hunt

BSE: Runs a dig pattern.

QB: After reverse pivoting and pretending to pitch to the aceback, sets deep, and reads the flat coverage first, the backside coverage second.

ACE: Goes into quick motion, stops abruptly as the ball is hiked, and blocks #1.

SB: Releases outside and runs flag route versus cover 2, and a 15-yard out versus all other coverages.

WB: Runs a five-yard drag.

PLAY #71

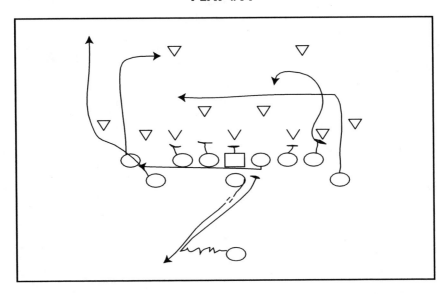

DESCRIPTION & BLOCKING RULES: This play is the quick pitch series' second play-action pass. **Bootleg pass blocking rules.**

COACHING POINTS: This pattern high-lows the frontside hook zone.

ASE: Runs a 15-yard in pattern.

AST: On, backside gap, hunt

ASG: On, backside gap, hunt

C: On, away

BSG: Pulls playside and blocks tandem, #1.

BST: Rule

BSE: Blocks #1 for two counts and finds a window in the backside hook zone.

QB: After reverse pivoting and pretending to pitch to the aceback, gains depth and fakes the aceback counter. Sets deep and reads the inside linebackers.

ACE: Goes into quick motion, but stops abruptly as the ball is hiked and directs his course toward the BSG. Fakes the aceback counter and blocks.

SB: Runs the wheel route.

WB: Runs a five-yard drag.

11

The Speed Option Series

Defense teams frequently attempt to play zero coverage versus the aceback offense, and augment their coverage with a heavy blitz package. Defenses that attempt this tactic leave themselves extremely vulnerable to the speed option. Aceback teams that can execute the speed option well will, therefore, either score a lot of points, or force the defense out of this pressure tactic.

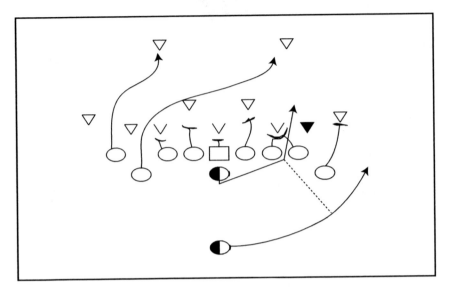

DESCRIPTION & BLOCKING RULES: This play, called the speed option, is what some coaches may refer to as the lead option. **Him option blocking rules.**

COACHING POINTS: The quarterback will option #1. If #1 attacks the quarterback, he will pitch to the aceback. If #1 plays the aceback, the quarterback will keep the ball.

ASE: Blocks #2

AST: Him

ASG: Him

C: Him

BSG: Him

BST: Him

BSE: Downfield

QB: Drop steps and options #1. Quarterback is aggressive; runs directly at #1; has the mental attitude that he is going to keep the ball. If he keeps it, plants on his downfield foot and immediately gets his shoulders parallel to the line of scrimmage. If he pitches it, makes a one-handed basketball pass from his heart to the aceback's heart.

ACE: Maintains a good pitch relationship with the quarterback. If the quarterback pitches the ball to him, locks it into his hands and immediately secures it. If the quarterback keeps it, turns up field with him and continues to maintain his pitch relationship because the quarterback may make the pitch downfield.

SB: Downfield

WB: Blocks the defensive back responsible for primary run support.

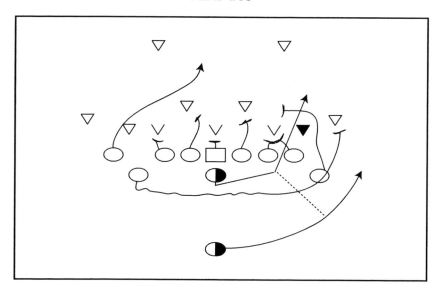

DESCRIPTION & BLOCKING RULES: This play is a variation of the speed option. **Him option blocking rules.**

COACHING POINTS: The wingback will influence #1 with the threat of a crack block. The wingback will then work to the next level and seal inside. Usually when #1 is influenced, he will fight to the outside in an attempt to maintain outside leverage. This tactic makes it easier for a good running quarterback to keep the ball. Some coaches may want to pull the backside guard to provide a lead blocker for the quarterback.

ASE: Blocks #2

AST: Him

ASG: Him

C: Him

BSG: Him

BST: Him

BSE: Downfield

QB: Drop steps and aggressively options #1 (same coaching points as Play #72).

ACE: He is the pitchback; maintains a good pitch relationship with the quarterback (same coaching points as Play #72).

SB: Goes into motion and blocks the defensive back responsible for primary run support.

WB: Influences #1, works to the second level, and seals pursuit.

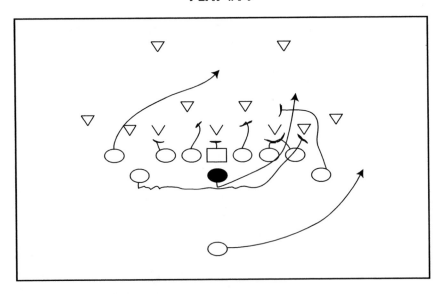

DESCRIPTION & BLOCKING RULES: This variation of the speed option is often referred to as a load option. **Him option blocking rules.**

COACHING POINTS: The wingback will influence #1 and then seal inside exactly as he did in Play #73. The slotback will go into motion and block #1. This should provide a sure running lane for the quarterback. The timing of the slotback's block is important; the wingback must have adequate time to influence #1 before the slotback makes his block.

ASE: Blocks #2

AST: Him

ASG: Him

C: Him

BSG: Him

BST: Him

BSE: Downfield

QB: Drop steps and aggressively options #1 (same coaching points as Play #72).

ACE: He is the pitchback; maintain a good pitch relationship with the quarterback (same coaching points as Play #72).

SB: Goes into motion and blocks #1. Kicks him out by blocking #1's inside hip with his right shoulder. If #1 plays the pitchback, SB blocks the cornerback.

WB: Influences #1, works to the second level, and seals pursuit.

PLAY #75

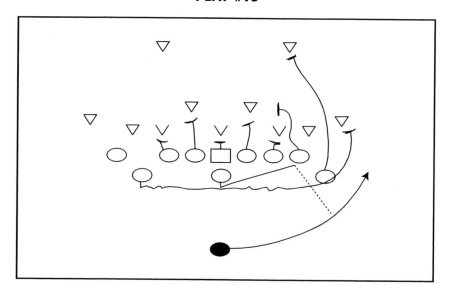

DESCRIPTION & BLOCKING RULES: This predetermined pitch to the tailback has an option look to it. **Him option blocking rules.**

COACHING POINTS: This play is most effective when the defense consistently has #1 play the quarterback.

ASE: Blocks #2 if he is playing a 7 technique. If #2 is playing a 5 technique, kiss blocks and then works to the next level to seal off pursuit.

AST: Him

ASG: Him

C: Him

BSG: Him

BST: Him

BSE: Downfield

QB: Drop steps and aggressively runs toward #1; convinces #1 that he intends to keep the ball. When #1 commits to him, he pitches the ball to the aceback.

ACE: Locks the ball into his hands and immediately secures it with his right hand. Finds the goal line and scores.

SB: Goes into motion and blocks the DB responsible for primary run support. Tries to attack this defender's outside hip with his left shoulder.

WB: Downfield

PLAY #76

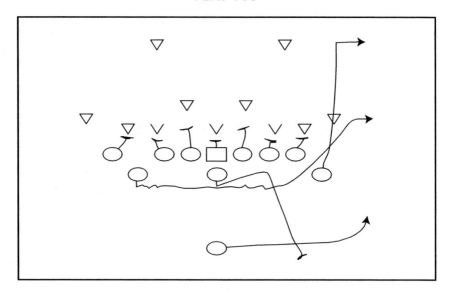

DESCRIPTION & BLOCKING RULES: This play-action pass takes advantage of the slotback's motion and the wingback's downfield release. **Standard pass pro blocking rules.**

COACHING POINT: The purpose of this pass is to high-low the flats.

ASE: Blocks #1

AST: On, backside gap, hunt

ASG: On, backside gap, hunt

C: On, backside gap, hunt

BSG: On, backside gap, hunt

BST: On, backside gap, hunt

BSE: Blocks #1 if he is inside of him. Runs a five-yard drag if #1 is outside of him.

QB: Drop steps and begins his option course. Just before he gets to the AST, drops straight back and reads the flat coverage.

ACE: Fakes the option, and runs a swing pattern.

SB: Goes into motion and runs a five-yard out.

WB: Releases as though he intends to block the DB responsible for primary run support. Brushes this defender's outside shoulder and runs a 15-yard out.

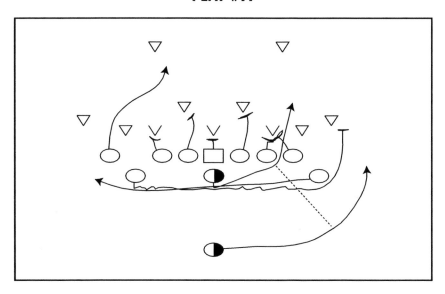

DESCRIPTION & BLOCKING RULES: This variation of the speed option fakes the reverse. **Variation of him option blocking rules.**

COACHING POINTS: Faking the reverse momentarily freezes secondary run support and sets the stage for the introduction of misdirection into the series.

ASE: Blocks #2

AST: Him

ASG: Him

C: Him

BSG: Him

BST: Him

BSE: Downfield

QB: Drop steps and aggressively options #1 (same coaching points as Play #72).

ACE: He is the pitchback; maintains a good pitch relationship with the quarterback (same coaching points as Play #72).

SB: Goes into motion and blocks the DB responsible for primary run support.

WB: Fakes the reverse.

PLAY #78

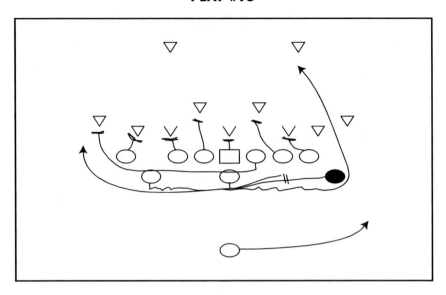

DESCRIPTION & BLOCKING RULES: This play is the reverse, the series' primary run-misdirection play. **Power blocking rules.**

COACHING POINTS: The quarterback must make sure that his drop step is deep enough to allow clearance for the pulling guard. The guard should also line up a little wider.

ASE: Inside, outside

AST: Rule

ASG: Rule

C: On, away

BSG: Pull and lead

BST: Fill

BSE: Fill inside

QB: Drop steps a little deeper than normal and begins his option course. He will not get very far because he will have to quickly deal the ball to the wingback.

ACE: Fakes the option.

SB: Goes into motion and blocks downfield.

WB: He is the ballcarrier. Quickly secures the ball into his left hand after receiving it from the quarterback, and reads the block of the pulling guard.

PLAY #79

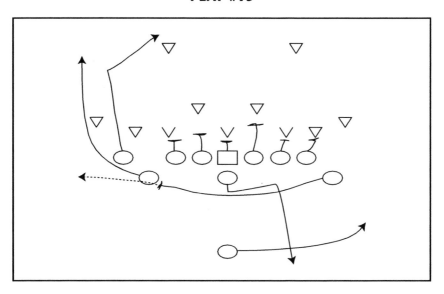

DESCRIPTION & BLOCKING RULES: This play-action pass employs misdirection. Standard pass pro blocking rules.

COACHING POINT: This throwback pattern exploits defensive pursuit.

ASE: Blocks #1

AST: On, backside gap, hunt

ASG: On, backside gap, hunt

C: On, backside gap, hunt

BSG: On, backside gap, hunt

BST: On, backside gap, hunt

BSE: Runs a skinny post versus cover 3, and a post versus all other coverages.

QB: Drop steps and begin his option course. Fakes the reverse, immediately drops straight back, and reads backside coverage.

ACE: Fakes the option and runs a swing pattern (he is the quarterback's outlet).

SB: Releases outside and streaks up the field.

WB: Fakes the reverse and blocks #1 backside. If #1 releases into coverage, runs a five-yard out into the flats.

PLAY #80

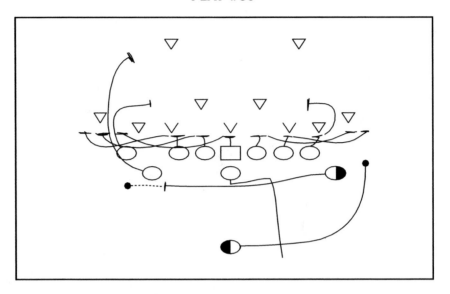

DESCRIPTION & BLOCKING RULES: This double-screen fakes the speed option reverse. **Standard pass pro blocking rules** (attackside is right).

COACHING POINTS: The line will follow their normal pass pro blocking rules for three counts and then release to their designated screen areas.

ASE: Blocks #1 for one-and-a-half counts, and then releases outside and seals off the inside linebacker.

AST: First, blocks on, backside gap, hunt, and then releases to his designated screen area.

ASG: First, blocks on, backside gap, hunt, and then releases to his designated screen area.

C: First, blocks on, backside gap, hunt, and then releases to his designated screen area.

BSG: First, blocks on, backside gap, hunt, and then releases to his designated screen area.

BST: First, blocks on, backside gap, hunt, and then releases to his designated screen area.

BSE: Releases outside and seals off the inside linebacker.

QB: Drop steps and begins his option course. Fakes the reverse, immediately drops straight back (slightly deeper than usual), and reads both flat coverages.

ACE: Fakes the option and as he sees the linemen release to their designated screen areas, releases to his spot behind the wall.

SB: Releases outside and blocks downfield.

WB: Fakes the reverse, momentarily blocks #1 backside, and then releases to his position behind the wall.

PLAY #81

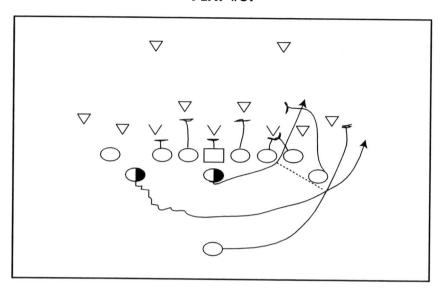

DESCRIPTION & BLOCKING RULES: This speed option, in which the slotback goes into motion and becomes the pitch man, employs the wingback threatening a crack block on #1. **Him option blocking rules.**

COACHING POINTS: Although not illustrated, the same concept could be established to the other side of the formation by sending the wingback into quick motion and using him as the pitchback.

ASE: Blocks #2

AST: Him

ASG: Him

C: Him

BSG: Him

BST: Him

BSE: Downfield

QB: Drop steps and aggressively options #1 (same coaching points as Play #72).

ACE: Arc releases and blocks the defensive back responsible for primary run support

SB: He is the pitchback. Goes into quick motion and immediately establishes a good pitch relationship with the quarterback. If the quarterback pitches the ball to him, he locks it into his hands and immediately secures it. If the quarterback keeps it, he turns upfield with him and continues to maintain his pitch relationship because the quarterback may make the pitch downfield.

WB: Influences #1, works to the second level, and seals pursuit.

12

The Iso Series

The iso series is another old series whose roots go back to Tom Nugent's I formation, and possibly even further back. Incorporated in the series are misdirection, option plays, play-action passes, and the strategic utilization of formations.

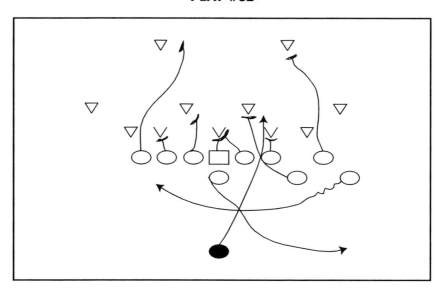

DESCRIPTION & BLOCKING RULES: The series' base play is iso. **Iso blocking rules.**

COACHING POINTS: By sending the wingback into quick motion, the offense is establishing misdirection. Because this is an inside play, it makes little difference to the offense how the defense adjusts its secondary to protect the flanks.

ASE: Downfield

AST: On, outside

ASG: On, reach, stack, inside

C: On, over, linebacker

BSG: On, over, backside gap

BST: On, over, backside gap

BSE: Downfield

QB: Steps straight back with his right foot. This will enable him to gain depth. As he steps, he immediately seats the ball. Next reverse pivots on his right foot and hands the ball to the aceback. Because he has seated the ball and turned his back to the defense, the ball has been hidden. Thus, he does not need to fake to the wingback, but he should simulate putting the ball on his right hip as he rolls out after the handoff.

ACE: Receives the ball from the quarterback and immediately secures it with both hands. Reads the blocks of both the BSG and SB.

SB: Blocks the inside linebacker.

WB: Goes into quick motion and fakes the reverse.

FAKE BIAST FIK RN

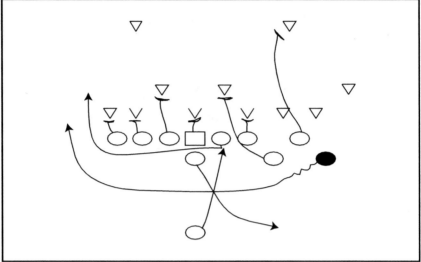

DESCRIPTION & BLOCKING RULES: This play is the iso reverse. **Punch blocking rules.**

COACHING POINTS: This is an excellent play when the defense plays corners-over versus trips. Versus this defense, a sucker play could easily be installed, using this blocking scheme, by having the quarterback give the ball to the aceback. The pulling guard would thus serve as a false key for the inside linebacker.

ASE: Blocks #1

AST: On, over, outside

ASG: On, over, reach, tandem, linebacker

C: Gap, on, away

BSG: Gap, pull, and lead

BST: Rule

BSE: Downfield

QB: Employs the same steps as he did on Play #82. Hands the ball to the wingback and fakes a bootleg away from the play.

ACE: Fakes the iso by running toward the hole with great intensity and slapping his left elbow with his right hand as he passes through the iso mesh point.

SB: Fills inside for the pulling guard.

WB: Goes into quick motion, receives the ball from the quarterback, and immediately secures it in his left hand. Reads the pulling guard's block as he approaches the perimeter.

FAKE BUST FKRU BAU

PLAY #84

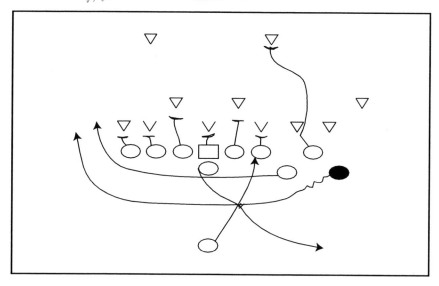

DESCRIPTION & BLOCKING RULES: This play is a variation of the iso reverse. **Base blocking rules.**

COACHING POINTS: This variation provides the defenders in the box no keys that a reverse is in progress. Like the previous reverse, a play could be devised in which the quarterback gives the ball to the aceback utilizing this backfield action and blocking scheme.

ASE: Blocks #1

AST: On, over, outside

ASG: On, over, reach, tandem, linebacker

C: Rule

BSG: Rule

BST: Rule

BSE: Downfield

QB: Employs the same steps as he did on Play #82. Hands the ball to the wingback and fakes a bootleg away from the play.

ACE: Fakes the iso by running toward the hole with great intensity and slapping his left elbow with his right hand as he passes through the iso mesh point.

SB: Pulls and leads the wingback around the corner.

WB: Goes into quick motion, receives the ball from the quarterback, and immediately secures it in his left hand. Reads the slotback's block as he approaches the perimeter.

PLAY #85

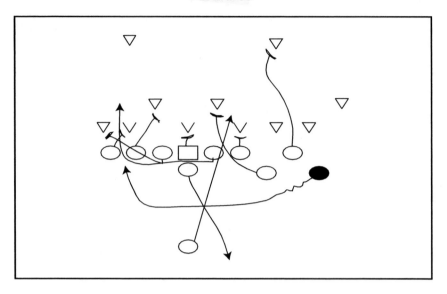

DESCRIPTION & BLOCKING RULES: This play is a fake iso off-tackle counter. **Slant blocking rules.**

COACHING POINTS: Like Play #83, the ball could be given to the aceback to create a sucker play.

ASE: Blocks #2

AST: Inside, linebacker

ASG: Pulls and traps #1

C: Gap, on, away

BSG: Gap, pull and lead

BST: Rule

BSE: Downfield

QB: Employs the same steps as he did on Play #82. Hands the ball to the wingback and fakes a bootleg away from the play.

ACE: Fakes the iso.

SB: Fills for the pulling guard.

WB: Goes into quick motion, receives the ball from the quarterback, and immediately secures it in his left hand. Reads the BSG's block as he blasts through the off-tackle hole.

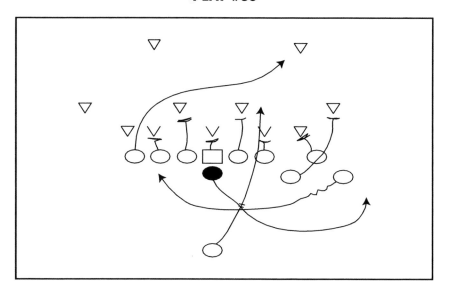

DESCRIPTION & BLOCKING RULES: This play is a bootleg keep. **Base blocking rules.**

COACHING POINTS: This variation provides the defenders in the box no keys regarding the play's direction. It is an excellent short yardage/red zone play. This variation is not a good call when the defense employs a corners-over secondary versus trips

ASE: Blocks #1

AST: On, over, outside

ASG: On, over, reach, tandem, linebacker

C: Rule

BSG: Rule

BST: Rule

BSE: Downfield

*FAKE FIK Rev
a R Keip*

QB: Employs the same steps as he did on Play #82. Fakes the ball to the wingback and hides it on his right hip as he races to the perimeter.

ACE: Fakes the iso. It is vital that he makes a great fake.

SB: Releases outside and blocks the DB responsible for primary run support.

WB: Goes into quick motion and fakes the reverse.

PLAY #87

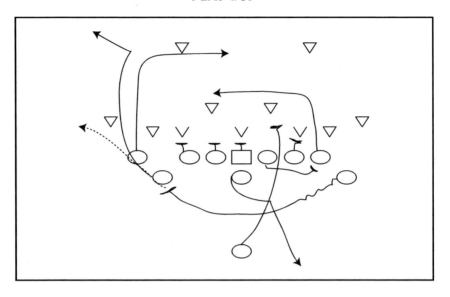

DESCRIPTION & BLOCKING RULES: This play-action pass utilizes an iso reverse fake. **Frontside pass blocking rules.**

COACHING POINT: This play-action pass high-lows the backside hook zones. Attackside is right.

ASE: Runs a five-yard drag.

AST: Inside, on

ASG: Pulls and blocks #1

C: On, frontside gap, hunt

BSG: On, frontside gap, hunt

BST: On, frontside gap, hunt

BSE: Runs a 15-yard in.

QB: Employs the same steps as he did on Play #82. Fakes the ball to the wingback, drops deep and reads the inside linebackers.

ACE: Fakes the iso and fills for the pulling guard.

SB: Releases outside and runs a flag pattern versus cover 2, and a post pattern versus all other coverages.

WB: Goes into quick motion and fakes the reverse and blocks #1 backside. If #1 drops into pass coverage, runs a five-yard out.

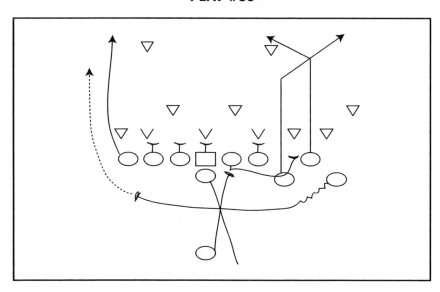

DESCRIPTION & BLOCKING RULES: This play-action pass utilizes an iso reverse fake. **Frontside pass blocking rules.**

COACHING POINT: This play-action pass attacks the deep sectors of the secondary. Attackside is right.

ASE: Runs a post pattern.

AST: Inside, on

ASG: Pulls and blocks #1

C: On, frontside gap, hunt

BSG: On, frontside gap, hunt

BST: On, frontside gap, hunt

BSE: Runs a skinny post.

QB: Employs the same steps as he did on Play #82. Fakes the ball to the wingback, drops deep and reads the safety(s).

ACE: Fakes the iso and fills for the pulling guard.

SB: Runs a flag pattern.

WB: Goes into quick motion, fakes the reverse, and blocks #1 backside. If #1 drops into pass coverage, trails the BSE upfield.

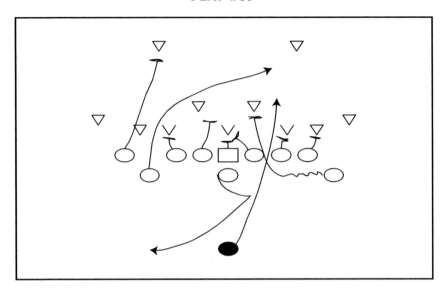

DESCRIPTION & BLOCKING RULES: This play is a variation of the iso in which the quarterback bootlegs away from the point of attack. **Iso blocking rules.**

COACHING POINTS: This play can be run with the illustrated motion or the quick motion illustrated in the seven previous plays. The advantage of this iso variation is that the aceback will read the AST's block and have the option of making either an inside or outside cut. Although not illustrated, a bootleg keep could be installed using this backfield action and punch blocking rules.

ASE: Downfield

AST: On, outside

ASG: On, reach, stack, inside

C: On, over, linebacker

BSG: On, over, backside gap

BST: On, over, linebacker

BSE: Downfield

QB: Steps as he did on the Play #82, makes the handoff, and then bootlegs away from the point of attack while pretending to hide the ball on his left hip.

ACE: Receives the ball from the quarterback and immediately secures it with both hands. Reads the AST's block and makes his cut accordingly.

SB: Downfield

WB: Goes into quick motion and blocks the inside linebacker.

PLAY #90

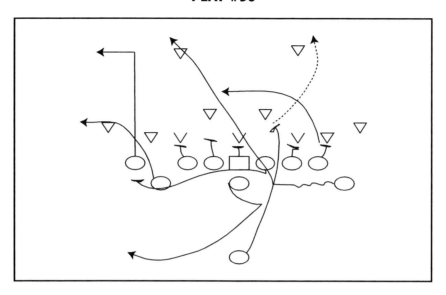

DESCRIPTION & BLOCKING RULES: This play-action pass employs iso bootleg action. **Bootleg pass blocking rules.**

COACHING POINTS: This pattern high-lows the flats zone. Attackside is left.

ASE: Runs a 15-yard out pattern.

AST: On, backside gap, hunt

ASG: On, backside gap, hunt

C: On, away

BSG: Pulls playside and blocks tandem, #1

BST: Rule

BSE: Blocks #1 for two counts and finds a window between the two inside linebackers.

QB: Steps as he did on Play #82, fakes the handoff, and then bootlegs away from the point of attack. Reads the flat coverage.

ACE: Fakes the iso and fills for the pulling guard. If everyone is blocked, rubs behind the BSE and streaks up the field.

SB: Releases outside and runs a five-yard out pattern.

WB: Goes into quick motion, sneaks through the line and attacks the playside deep third.

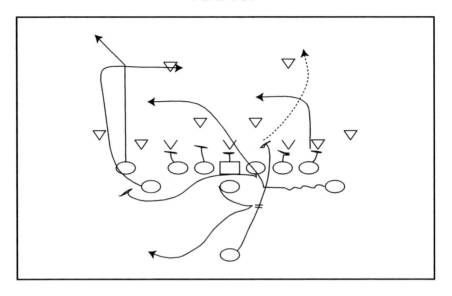

DESCRIPTION & BLOCKING RULES: This is another play-action pass that employs iso bootleg action. **Bootleg pass blocking rules.**

COACHING POINTS: This pattern high-lows the hook zone. Attackside is left.

ASE: Runs a flag pattern versus cover 2, and a post pattern versus all other coverages.

AST: On, backside gap, hunt

ASG: On, backside gap, hunt

C: On, away

BSG: Pulls playside and blocks, Tandem, #1

BST: Rule

BSE: Blocks #1 for two counts and finds a window between the two inside linebackers.

QB: Step as he did on the Play #82, fakes the handoff, and then bootlegs away from the point of attack. Reads the flat coverage.

ACE: Fakes the iso and fills for the pulling guard. If no one is there to block, streaks upfield.

SB: Releases outside and runs a 15-yard in pattern.

WB: Goes into quick motion, sneaks through the line, and runs a five-yard out.

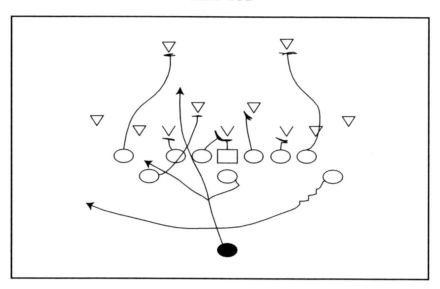

DESCRIPTION & BLOCKING RULES: This play is the final version of the iso. **Iso blocking rules.**

COACHING POINTS: The purpose of this variation is to set up the iso option. The quarterback will need to adjust his footwork to execute this play successfully.

ASE: Downfield

AST: On, outside

ASG: On, reach, stack, inside

C: On, over, linebacker

BSG: On, over, backside gap

BST: On, over, linebacker

BSE: Downfield

QB: Steps sideways with his right foot and then steps back with his left foot so that his shoulders are perpendicular to the line of scrimmage. Hands the ball to the aceback, then runs directly at #1 and simulates the option.

ACE: Receives the ball from the quarterback and immediately secures it with both hands. Reads the blocks of both the BSG and SB.

SB: Blocks the inside linebacker.

WB: Goes into quick motion and fakes the option.

PLAY #93

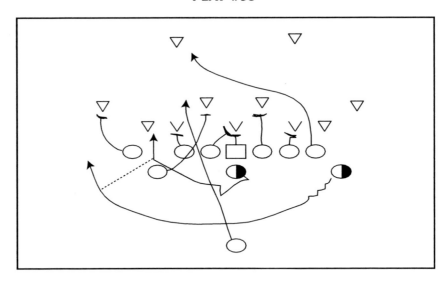

DESCRIPTION & BLOCKING RULES: This play is the final play of the iso option series. **Iso blocking rules.**

COACHING POINTS: It is vital that the quarterback runs toward the line of scrimmage in executing the option, and not run downhill.

ASE: Releases outside and blocks the defensive back responsible for primary and secondary support.

AST: On, outside

ASG: On, reach, stack, inside

C: On, over, linebacker

BSG: On, over, backside gap

BST: On, over, linebacker

BSE: Downfield

QB: Steps sideways with his right foot, and then steps back with his left foot so that his shoulders are perpendicular to the line of scrimmage. Fakes to the aceback and then options #1. Quarterback should be aggressive; runs directly at #1. If he keeps the ball, quarterback plants on his downfield foot and immediately gets his shoulders parallel to the line of scrimmage. If he pitches it, he makes a one-handed basketball pass from his heart to the aceback's heart.

ACE: Fakes the iso.

SB: Blocks the inside linebacker.

WB: He is the pitchback. Goes into quick motion and establishes a good pitch relationship with the quarterback. If the quarterback pitches the ball to him, WB looks it into his hands and immediately secures it in his left hand. If the quarterback keeps it, WB turns upfield with him and continues to maintain his pitch relationship because the quarterback may make the pitch downfield.

13

The Buck Sweep Series

This series is an adaptation of the wing-T. Although only four plays have been included in this chapter, almost any wing-T play can be remade into a bunch play. The plays in this chapter begin with a quick-hitting slotback sweep followed by an aceback counter trey in the direction of the sweep.

PLAY #94

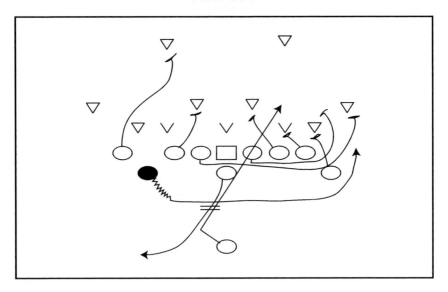

DESCRIPTION & BLOCKING RULES: This play is the slotback buck sweep. **Bounce blocking rules.**

COACHING POINTS: The counter trey action toward the direction of the sweep accomplishes the same objectives as the wing-T's fullback trap.

ASE: Inside, linebacker

AST: Inside, linebacker

ASG: Pulls and leads, looks for the inside linebacker.

C: Gap, on, away

BSG: Gap, pull and lead

BST: Fill

BSE: Downfield

QB: Opens up toward the slotback, hands him the ball, and then fakes the aceback counter trey before bootlegging away from the point of attack.

ACE: Crosses over step with his right foot, steps with his left foot, plants and pivots on this step, and fakes the counter trey.

SB: Goes into quick motion, receives the handoff from the quarterback, secures the ball with his right hand, and reads the block of the BSG.

WB: Blocks #1

PLAY #95

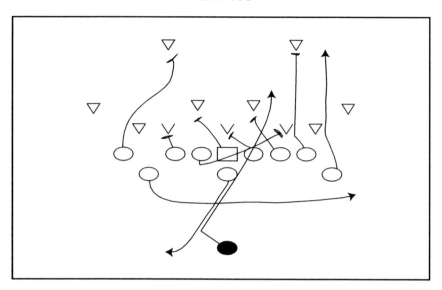

DESCRIPTION & BLOCKING RULES: This play is the counter trey (without the pull and lead of the BST) that complements the slotback buck sweep. **Him trap blocking rules.**

COACHING POINTS: The AST's down-block and ASE's influence puts the 5 technique in a double bind: fight outside to stop the buck sweep or close inside to stop the counter trey?

ASE: Influences inside and then blocks downfield.

AST: Him

ASG: Him

C: Him

BSG: Him

BST: Him

BSE: Downfield

QB: Opens up toward the slotback, fakes the sweep, and then hands the ball to the aceback. Fakes the bootleg away from the point of attack by pretending to hide the ball on his left hip.

ACE: Crosses over step with his right foot, steps with his left foot, plants and pivots on this step, receives the handoff, and immediately secures the ball with both hands.

SB: Goes into quick motion and fakes the buck sweep.

WB: Influences #1 and blocks downfield.

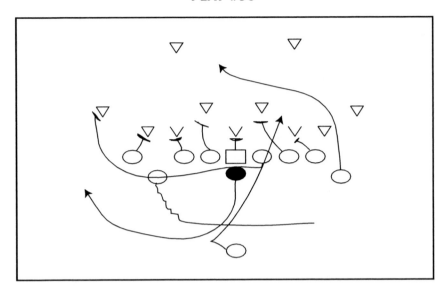

DESCRIPTION & BLOCKING RULES: This play is the quarterback bootleg run. **Punch blocking rules.**

COACHING POINTS: The quarterback needs to set up this play himself by making great fakes on the buck sweep and counter trey.

ASE: Inside

AST: On, over, outside

ASG: On, over, reach, tandem, linebacker

C: Gap, on, away

BSG: Gap, pull and lead through the C gap

BST: Fill

BSE: Fill inside

QB: Opens up toward the slotback and fakes the sweep. Does not worry about faking the counter trey. Hides the ball on his left hip and reads the guard's block as he approaches the perimeter.

ACE: Fakes the counter trey by slapping his left elbow with his right hand as he passes through the counter trey mesh point.

SB: Goes into quick motion and fakes the buck sweep.

WB: Downfield

PLAY #97

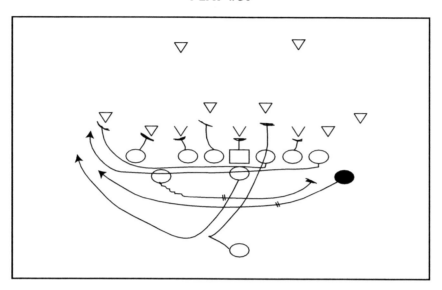

DESCRIPTION & BLOCKING RULES: This play is the buck sweep reverse. **Variation of punch blocking rules.**

COACHING POINTS: This play needs a couple of practice reps each day to perfect the ballhandling skills. It is an excellent reverse because of the number of blockers it gets in front of the ballcarrier.

ASE: Inside

AST: On, over, outside

ASG: On, over, reach, tandem, linebacker

C: Gap, on, away

BSG: Gap, pull and lead

BST: Fill

BSE: Pull and lead

QB: Opens up toward the slotback and hands him the ball. Does not worry about faking the counter trey. Pretends to hide the ball on his left hip as he fakes the bootleg for a few steps before leading the wingback around end.

ACE: Fakes the counter trey by slapping his left elbow with his right hand as he passes through the counter trey mesh point.

SB: Goes into quick motion, receives the handoff from the quarterback and immediately shifts the ball into his right hand. Gently gives the ball to the wingback. Slamming the ball into the wingback's pouch is a possible cause of fumbles.

WB: He is the ballcarrier. Receives the handoff from the slotback and immediately secures it in his left hand. Reads the blocks of the tight end and quarterback as he approaches the perimeter.

PLAY #98

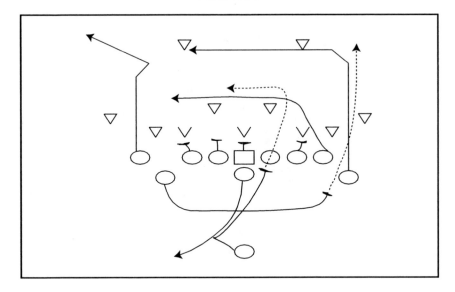

DESCRIPTION & BLOCKING RULES: This bootleg pass is the last play of the series. **Bootleg pass blocking rules.**

COACHING POINTS: This play is very similar to the wing-T bootleg pass.

ASE: Runs a smash pattern.

AST: On, backside gap, hunt

ASG: On, backside gap, hunt

C: On, away

BSG: Pulls playside and blocks tandem, #1.

BST: Rule

BSE: Runs a five-yard drag.

QB: Opens up toward the slotback and fakes the buck sweep. Does not worry about faking the counter trey. Momentarily hides the ball on his left hip as he executes the bootleg. Reads the inside linebackers and flat coverage.

ACE: Fakes the counter trey and then blocks for the pulling guard. If no one shows, finds a window between the two inside linebackers.

SB: Goes into quick motion, fakes the buck sweep, and then blocks #1 backside. If #1 drops into coverage, streaks up the field.

WB: Runs a dig pattern.

14

The Draw Series

The Draw Series is the final series. Although only three plays will be presented in this chapter, the drop pass play possibilities, employing fake draw action, are countless.

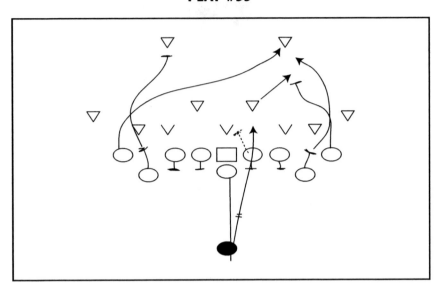

DESCRIPTION & BLOCKING RULES: This play is the draw play. **Him blocking rules.**

COACHING POINTS: All linemen will show pass at the snap. Versus the 3-4, the ASG will block the inside linebacker if he blitzes. If the linebacker drops into coverage, the ASG will double-team the nose tackle with the center.

ASE: Releases downfield and blocks the inside linebacker if he drops into coverage. If the linebacker blitzes, block downfield.

AST: Him

ASG: Him

C: Him

BSG: Him

BST: Him

BSE: Downfield

QB: Drops straight back and hands the ball to the aceback.

ACE: Takes a shuffle step to his right and momentarily shows intent to block. Waits for the quarterback, receives the ball, and reads the ASG's and ASE's blocks.

SB: Slams #1 and then releases downfield.

WB: Slams #1 and then releases downfield.

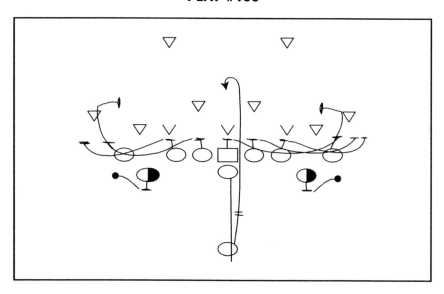

DESCRIPTION & BLOCKING RULES: This play is a double screen that is initiated by the fake draw. **Standard pass pro blocking rules.**

COACHING POINTS: The line will follow their normal pass pro blocking rules for three counts and then release to their designated screen areas.

ASE: Releases outside and seals the inside linebacker.

AST: First blocks on, backside gap, hunt, and then releases to his designated screen area.

ASG: First blocks on, backside gap, hunt, and then releases to his designated screen area.

C: First blocks on, backside gap, hunt, and then releases to his designated screen area.

BSG: First blocks on, backside gap, hunt, and then releases to his designated screen area.

BST: First blocks on, backside gap, hunt, and then releases to his designated screen area.

BSE: Releases outside and seals the inside linebacker.

QB: Drops straight back, fakes the draw, and reads the inside linebackers.

ACE: Takes a shuffle step to his right and momentarily shows intent to block. Waits for the quarterback, fakes the draw. If he does not get tackled, finds a window between the two inside linebackers.

SB: Blocks for three counts, and then releases to his position behind the wall.

WB: Blocks for three counts, and then releases to his position behind the wall.

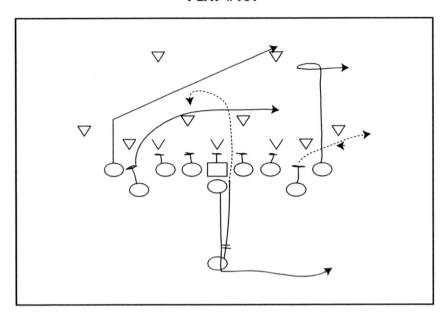

DESCRIPTION & BLOCKING RULES: This play-action pass fakes the draw and features quarterback dash action. **Standard pass pro blocking rules.**

COACHING POINTS: It is important that both the quarterback and aceback make great fakes and convince the defense that a draw is in progress. Attackside is right.

ASE: Turns a 15-yard curl and out.

AST: On, backside gap, hunt

ASG: On, backside gap, hunt

C: On, backside gap, hunt

BSG: On, backside gap, hunt

BST: On, backside gap, hunt

BSE: Runs a post.

QB: Drops straight back, fakes the draw, dashes to the right, and reads the flat coverage.

ACE: Takes a shuffle step to his right and momentarily shows intent to block. Waits for the quarterback, receives the ball, and fakes the draw. If he does not get tackled, finds a window between the two inside linebackers.

SB: Slams #1 and then runs a five-yard drag.

WB: Blocks #1. If he releases into coverage, runs a five-yard out into the flats.

15

Illustrated
Blocking Assignments

POWER BLOCKING RULES
(Attackside is right.)

PLAYS USING THESE RULES	ASSIGNMENT REVIEW
1, 2, 3, 19, 58, 69, 78	**ASE:** Blocks #2
	AST: Rule
	ASG: Rule
	C: On, away
	BSG: Pull and lead
	BST: Fill
	BSE: Downfield
	SB: Goes into motion and kicks out #1.
	WB: Executes the option called in the huddle.

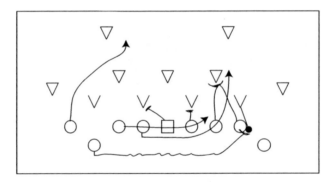

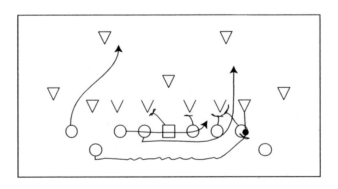

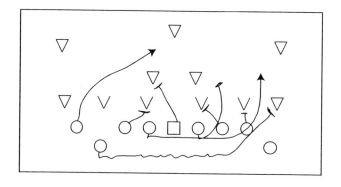

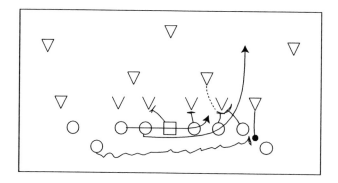

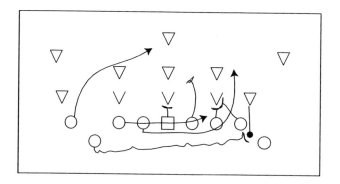

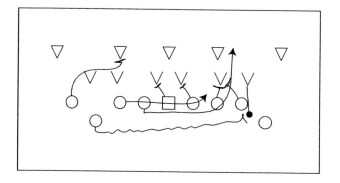

BOUNCE BLOCKING RULES

(Attackside is right.)

PLAYS USING THESE RULES	ASSIGNMENT REVIEW
4, 6, 7, 35, 59, 67, 94	**ASE:** Inside, linebacker
	AST: Inside, linebacker
	ASG: Pull and lead, looks for the inside LB.
	C: Gap, on, away
	BSG: Gap, pull and lead
	BST: Fill
	BSE: Downfield
	SB: Depends upon play
	WB: Blocks #1, caves him inside.

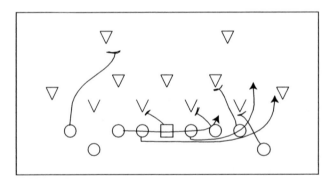

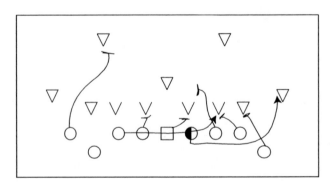

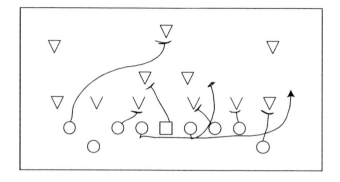

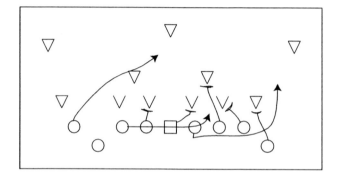

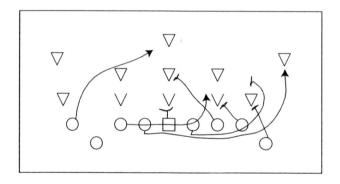

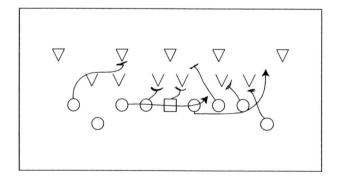

WEAKSIDE POWER BLOCKING RULES

(Attackside is left.)

PLAYS USING THESE RULES	ASSIGNMENT REVIEW
5, 16, 54	**ASE:** Inside, linebacker
	AST: Rule
	ASG: Rule
	C: On, away
	BSG: Pull and lead
	BST: Fill
	BSE: Downfield
	SB: Depends upon play
	WB: Depends upon play

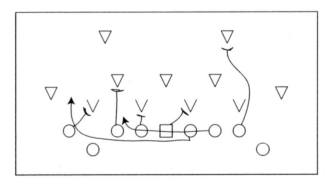

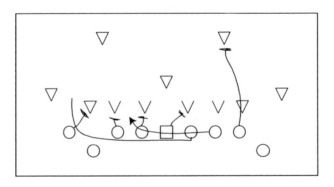

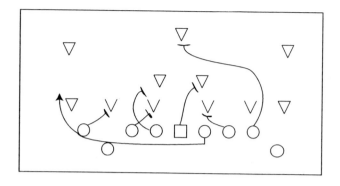

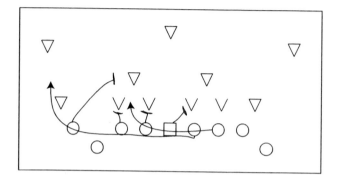

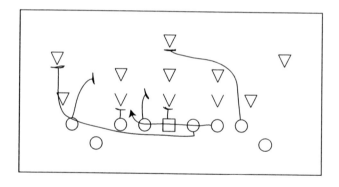

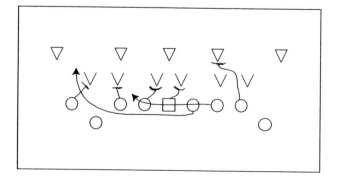

STANDARD PASS PRO BLOCKING RULES

(Attackside is right.)

PLAYS USING THESE RULES	ASSIGNMENT REVIEW
8, 9, 10, 12, 13, 17, 28, 30, 41, 42, 43, 45, 50, 51, 52, 55, 64, 70, 76, 79, 80, 100, 101	**ASE:** Depends upon play **AST:** On, backside gap, hunt **ASG:** On, backside gap, hunt **C:** On, backside gap, hunt **BSG:** On, backside gap, hunt **BST:** On, backside gap, hunt **ASE:** Depends upon play

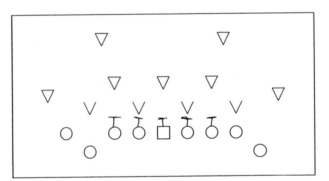

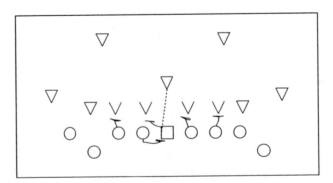

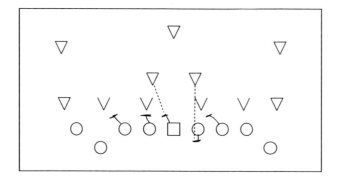

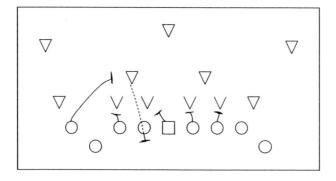

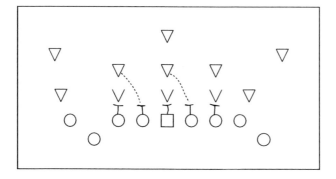

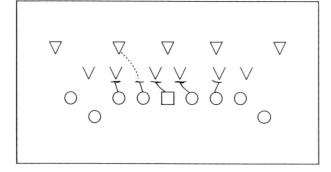

COUNTER BLOCKING RULE
(Attackside is left.)

PLAYS USING THESE RULES	ASSIGNMENT REVIEW
11	**ASE:** Downfield
	AST: If the ASG is covered, blocks on, over, outside. If the ASG is uncovered, blocks linebacker.
	ASG: Inside, linebacker (exception: split-4)
	C: Away (exception: split-4)
	BSG: Pull and trap
	BST: On, over, outside
	BSE: Pull and lead
	SB: Goes into motion and blocks #1.
	WB: Ballcarrier

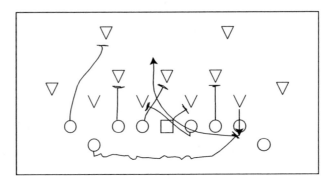

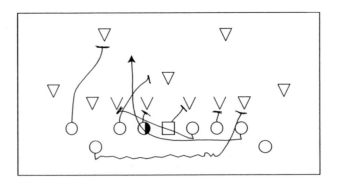

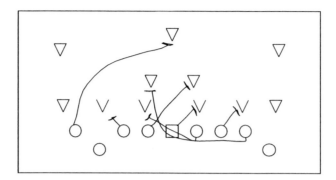

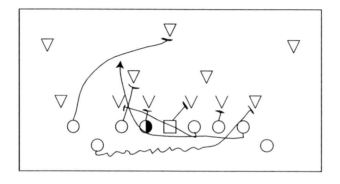

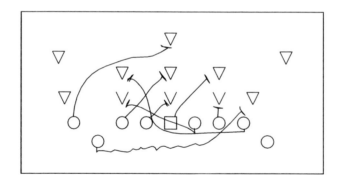

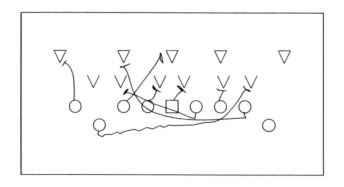

OTIS BLOCKING RULES

(Attackside is left.)

PLAYS USING THESE RULES	ASSIGNMENT REVIEW
14, 15, 27, 33, 48, 66	**ASE:** Downfield
	AST: If ASG is covered, blocks on, over, outside. If ASG is uncovered, blocks linebacker.
	ASG: Inside, linebacker (exception: split-4)
	C: Away (exception: split-4)
	BSG: Pull and trap
	BST: Pull and lead
	BSE: Fills inside.
	SB: Depends upon play
	WB: Depends upon play

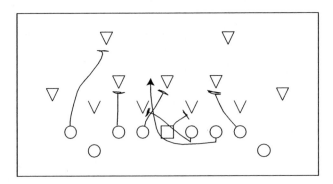

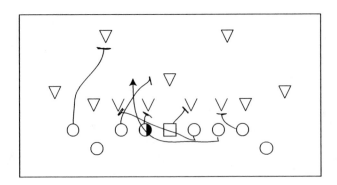

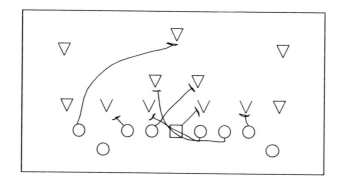

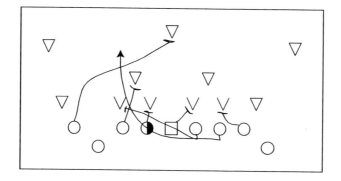

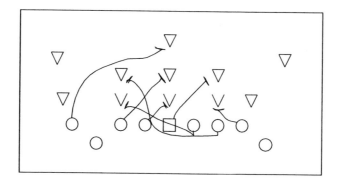

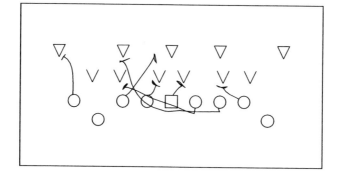

HIM TRAP BLOCKING RULES
(Attackside is right.)

PLAYS USING THESE RULES	ASSIGNMENT REVIEW
18, 34, 61, 95	**ASE:** Him
	AST: Him
	ASG: Him
	C: Him
	BSG: Him
	BST: Him
	BSE: Him
	SB: Depends upon play
	WB: Depends upon play

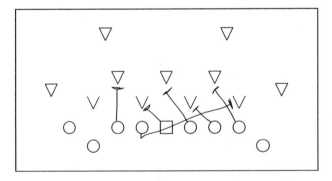

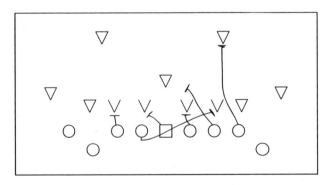

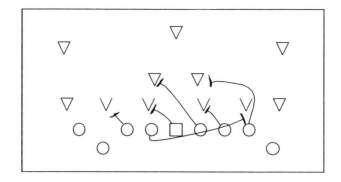

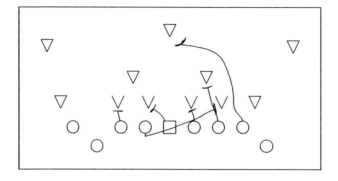

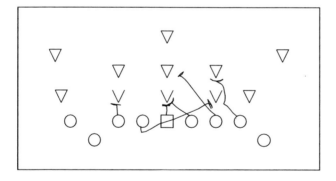

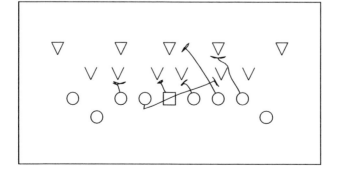

PUNCH BLOCKING RULES

(Attackside is left.)

PLAYS USING THESE RULES	ASSIGNMENT REVIEW
20, 25, 31, 49, 53, 57, 83, 96, 97	**ASE:** Blocks #1
	AST: On, over, outside
	ASG: On, over, reach, tandem, linebacker
	C: Gap, on, away
	BSG: Gap, pull and lead
	BST: Fills inside.
	BSE: Depends upon play
	SB: Depends upon play
	WB: Depends upon play

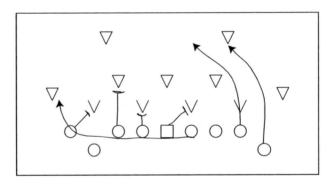

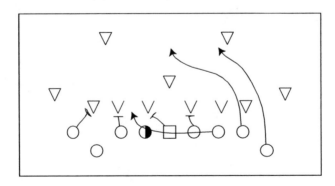

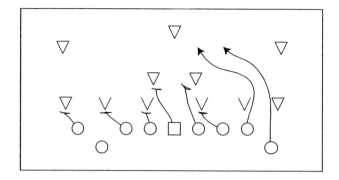

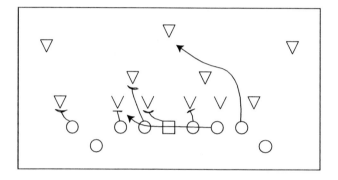

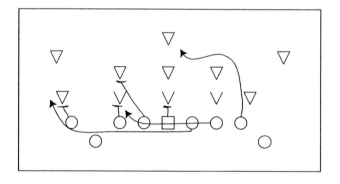

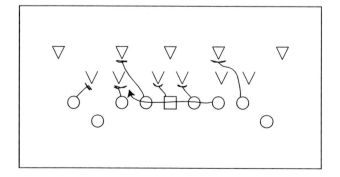

BASE BLOCKING RULES
(Attackside is right.)

PLAYS USING THESE RULES	ASSIGNMENT REVIEW
22, 29, 32, 37, 38, 40, 46, 47, 84, 86	**ASE:** Blocks #1
	AST: On, over, outside
	ASG: On, over, reach, tandem, linebacker
	C: Rule
	BSG: Rule
	BST: Rule
	BSE: Downfield
	SB: Depends upon play
	WB: Depends upon play

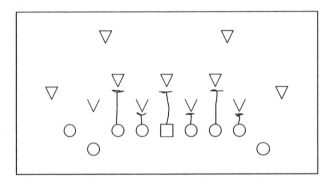

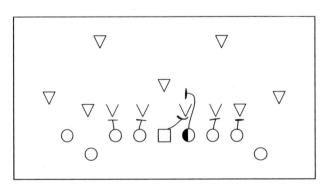

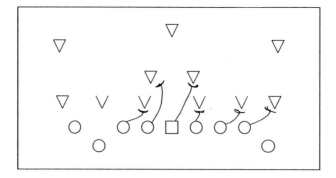

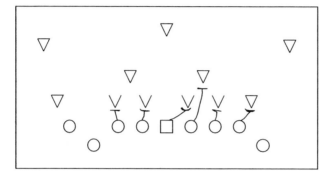

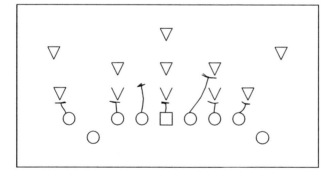

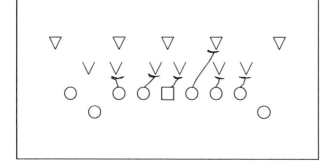

SLANT BLOCKING RULES
(Attackside is right.)

PLAYS USING THESE RULES	ASSIGNMENT REVIEW
23, 24, 60, 62, 63, 85	**ASE:** Blocks #2
	AST: Inside, linebacker
	ASG: Pulls and traps #1
	C: Gap, on, away
	BSG: Gap, pull and lead
	BST: Fills if the guard pulls; otherwise, blocks rule
	BSE: Downfield
	SB: Downfield
	WB: Tandem, downfield (if attackside)

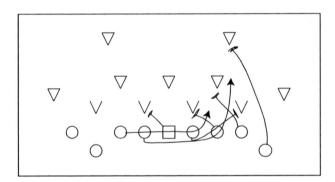

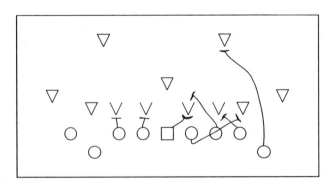

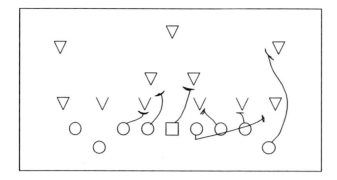

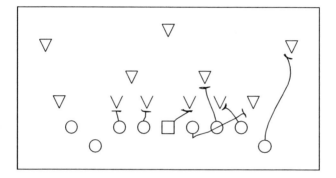

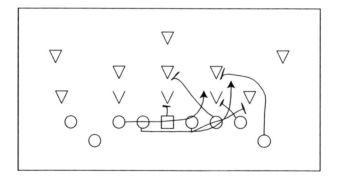

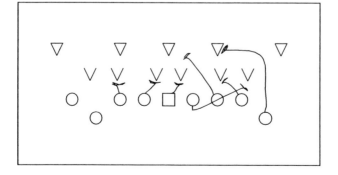

BOOTLEG PASS BLOCKING RULES

(Attackside is right.)

PLAYS USING THESE RULES	ASSIGNMENT REVIEW
21, 26, 36, 71, 90, 91, 98	**ASE:** Depends on play
	AST: On, backside gap, hunt
	ASG: On, backside gap, hunt
	C: On, away
	BSG: Pulls playside and blocks tandem, #1.
	BST: Rule
	BSE: Depends on play
	SB: Depends on play
	WB: Depends on play

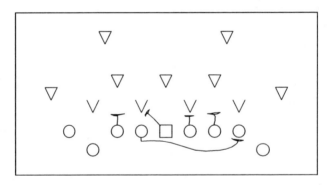

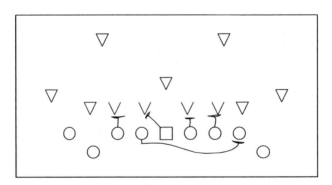

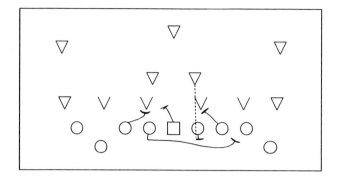

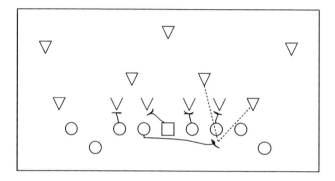

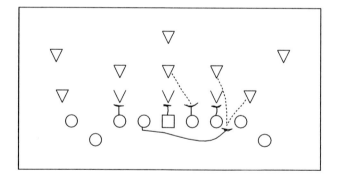

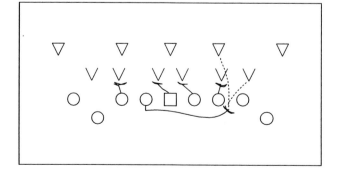

HIM BLOCKING RULES
(Attackside is right.)

PLAYS USING THESE RULES	ASSIGNMENT REVIEW
39, 44, 99	**ASE:** Releases and blocks inside linebacker.
	AST: Him
	ASG: Him
	C: Him
	BSG: Him
	BST: Him
	BSE: Depends upon play
	SB: Depends upon play
	WB: Depends upon play

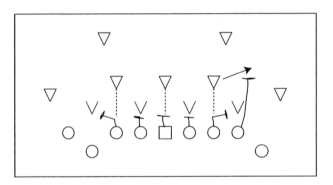

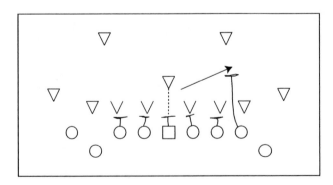

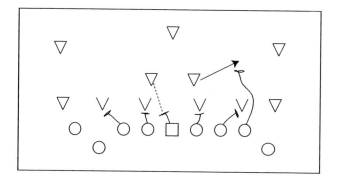

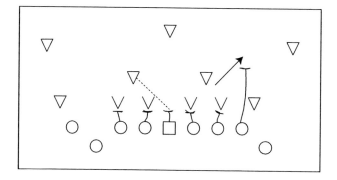

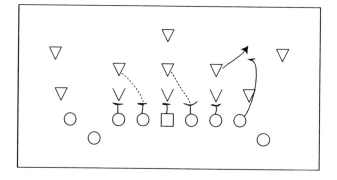

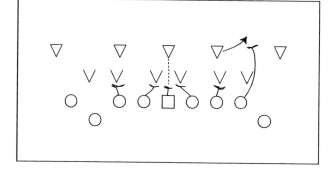

TACKLE TRAP BLOCKING RULES
(Attackside is left.)

PLAYS USING THESE RULES	ASSIGNMENT REVIEW
56	**ASE:** Downfield
	AST: Over, tandem, linebacker
	ASG: Gap, stack, inside, linebacker
	C: On, over, away
	BSG: On, over, backside gap, tandem
	BST: Pull and trap
	BSE: Fills inside.
	SB: Depends upon play
	WB: Depends upon play

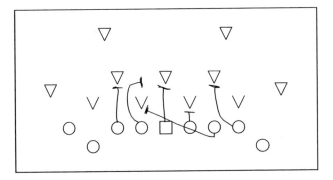

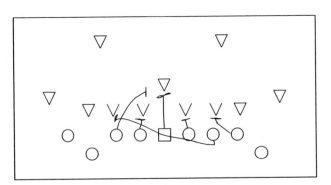

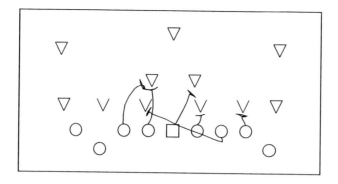

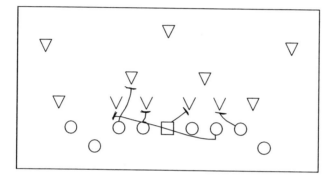

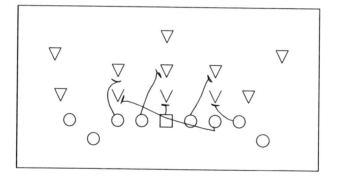

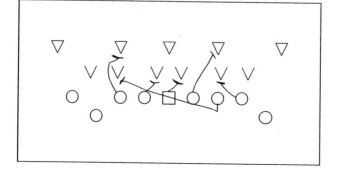

HIM OPTION BLOCKING RULES

(Attackside is right.)

PLAYS USING THESE RULES	ASSIGNMENT REVIEW
72, 73, 74, 75, 77, 81	**ASE:** Blocks #2
	AST: Him
	ASG: Him
	C: Him
	BSG: Him
	BST: Him
	BSE: Downfield
	SB: Depends on play
	WB: Depends on play

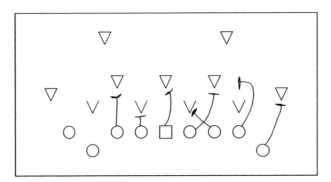

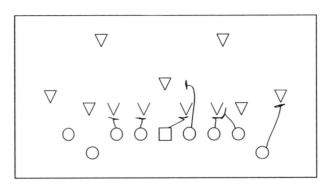

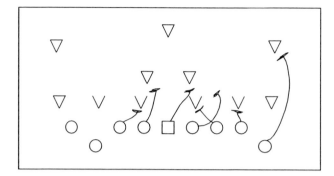

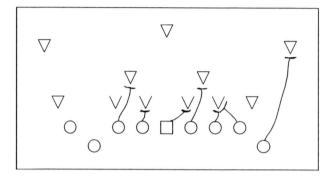

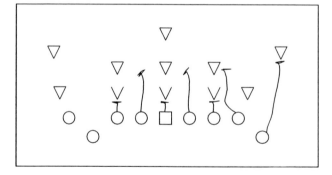

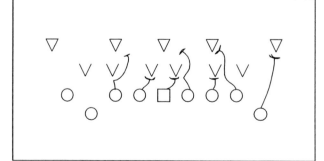

ISO BLOCKING RULES

(Attackside is right.)

PLAYS USING THESE RULES	ASSIGNMENT REVIEW
82, 89, 92, 93	**ASE:** Depends on play
	AST: On, outside
	ASG: On, reach, stack, inside
	C: On, over, linebacker
	BSG: On, over, backside gap
	BST: On, over, backside gap
	BSE: Depends on play
	SB: Depends on play
	WB: Depends on play

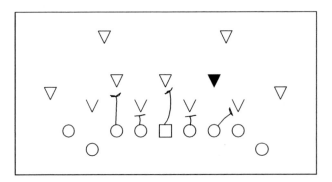

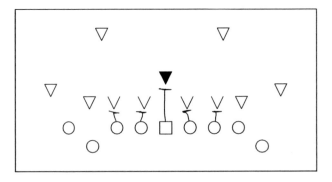

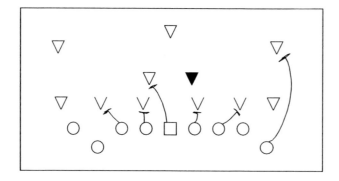

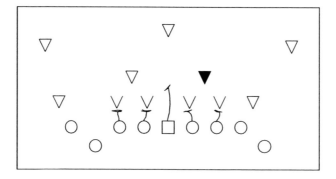

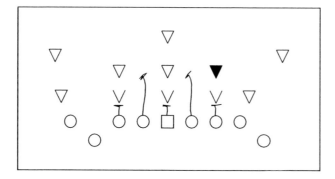

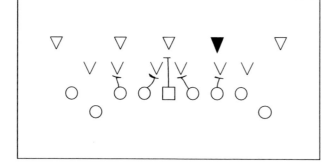

FRONTSIDE PASS BLOCKING RULES

(Attackside is right.)

PLAYS USING THESE RULES	ASSIGNMENT REVIEW
87, 88	**ASE:** Runs designated pattern.
	AST: Inside, on
	ASG: Pulls and blocks #1
	C: On, frontside gap, hunt
	BSG: On, frontside gap, hunt
	BST: On, frontside gap, hunt
	BSE: Runs designated pattern.
	SB: Runs designated pattern.
	WB: Goes into quick motion and blocks backside.

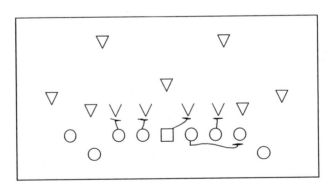

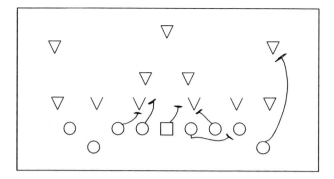

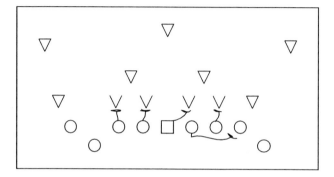

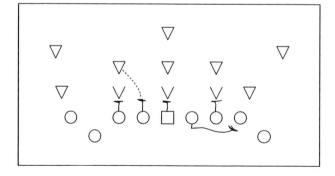

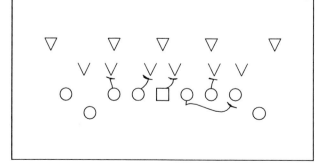

About the Author

Leo Hand is the defensive backfield coach at Andress High School in El Paso, Texas, a position he assumed in 2004. Previously, he served as the defensive coordinator at El Paso (TX) High School from 2001 to 2003. Prior to that, he held the same job at Irvin High School in El Paso, Texas. With over 33 years of experience as a teacher and coach, Hand has served in a variety of coaching positions in his career. At each stop, he has achieved a notable level of success.

A graduate of Emporia State University in Emporia, Kansas, Hand began his football coaching career in 1968 as the junior varsity coach at McQuaid Jesuit High School in Rochester, New York. After two seasons, he then accepted the job as the offensive line coach at Aquinas Institute (1970-'71). Next, he served as the head coach at Saint John Fisher College—a position he held for two years. He has also served on the gridiron staffs at APW (Parrish, NY) High School (head coach); Saint Anthony (Long Beach, CA) High School (head coach), Daniel Murphy (Los Angeles, CA) High School (head coach), Servite (Anaheim, CA) High School (head coach); Serra (Gardena, CA) High School (head coach); Long Beach (CA) City College (offensive line and linebackers); and Los Angeles (CA) Harbor College (offensive coordinator).

During the last six years that he spent coaching interscholastic teams in California, Hand's squads won 81 percent of their games in the highly competitive area of Southern California. At Serra High School, his teams compiled a 24-1 record, won a CIF championship, and were declared California State champions. On numerous occasions, he has helped rebuild several floundering gridiron teams into highly successful programs. For his efforts, he has been honored on numerous occasions with Coach of the Year recognition.

A former Golden Gloves boxing champion, Hand is a prolific author, having written several football instructional books and numerous articles that have been published. He and his wife, Mary, have nine children and eleven grandchildren.